The Teen Transformation Manual

The Teen Transformation Manual

Maya Cointreau

An Earth Lodge® Publication
Wallingford, Vermont

More Earth Lodge® Books

Table of Contents

Introduction

Everybody always says that change is never easy, but that's an old paradigm.

Change is beautiful.

Change is exciting.

Change is natural.

Grownups like to talk about how hard it is to change jobs or move to a new house, but you're going through one of the toughest transformations there is: you're changing from a child to an adult. Your body is developing new hormonal and nervous system response mechanisms. Your brain is being completely re-wired with millions of new connections that will eventually help you evaluate risks and make great decisions. While your body changes and grows, you need more sleep and time to relax than ever before so that you can adjust to your ever-evolving state of being. AND you're still expected to go to school and take on more chores. Get a job. Decide what you want to do for the rest of your life. Now that's stressful. That's real change.

That's why I'm writing this book for you. I remember how hard it was to be a teen, and I've watched my own kids go through the process, too. Now, more than ever, you can use some extra support. This manual is meant to be a lifeline, filled with techniques you can use to navigate everything life throws at you – whether you choose to start using all the tools here or just one each week. Each chapter will build upon the ones before it, taking you through easy ways to feel more comfortable every day, no matter what life throws at you, to more advanced techniques that will help you find your way to a life path that is truly satisfying, body and soul. The best part? You'll start your journey as a young adult with a full set of wings that will fly you wherever you want to go. You might be the only person who can see them, but that's all that matters. You'll know they're there. You'll be strong of mind, self-assured, and confident with the whole support of Source behind you.

What's that? What is Source? Well, it's like God, except it's YOU. We've all heard the saying "God is everywhere." Few really understand what that means but I guarantee that by the time you finish this book, you'll get it. Source is the beginning and end of everything that is, and everything in between, too. It is the Qi or Prana that animates your body, the breath of life that created you. It is the core of all matter, space and time at a quantum level where everything is one and the same, where everything is simply vibrations in the void.

In practical terms, Source is your higher self or soul, as well as its origin point.

Source is the higher wisdom of our guides and angels, of gods and goddesses, of our ancestors who have passed into the light, the collective being-ness of all non-physical reality. Hard to define, but Spirit doesn't care about definitions. It's all around us, flowing through us and between us at all times.

It is everything. And so, it is you. You are Source. You are a god within your own body. It's time for you to get comfortable with yourself and claim your power.

Time to transform and fly!

Breathe Easy

Before we go any further, it's a good idea to take a moment to slow ourselves down so we can process the world more clearly. One of the easiest ways to do that is to pay attention to your breathing, making a conscious effort to breathe more deeply and completely. Most people don't breathe the way they're bodies intended. Pretty shocking, right? It's something you do every minute of every day, but chances are you forgot how to breathe the right way somewhere after toddlerhood. Babies know how to rock their lungs — next time you're around one, watch how its belly fills up every time it breathes in. Instead of taking shallow breaths that lift the chest, young kids fill their lungs ALL the way, using their diaphragm to pull air deep down. The deeper you breathe, the more oxygen your body processes with each breath, strengthening your lungs, increasing stamina and fueling all your cells. Want to get strong? Practice breathing!

First, put one hand on your stomach, just above your belly button. That's where your diaphragm lives, stretching across from one side to the other beneath your abs. Next, out the other on your upper chest, below your collarbone. When you breathe in and out, your lower hand should be rising and falling while the hand on your chest hardly moves. If they are doing the opposite, you're not using your diaphragm! Shallow breathing is bad for the body and weakens the lungs. Practice diaphragm breathing until your belly and your lower hand is moving up and down easily.

Now, let's start with the **Four-Fold Breath**.

It's simple. So simple, in fact, that you can do it in class, at the dinner table, or on the bus.

Breathe in for a count of four.

Hold your breath for a count of four.

Exhale for a count of four.

Wait (Don't breathe in yet!) for a count of four.

Breathe in...2...3...4

Hold...2...3...4

Exhale...2...3...4

Wait...2...3...4

Breathe in...2...3...4

Hold...2...3...4

Exhale...2...3...4

Wait...2...3...4

You can count as slowly or quickly as you like — the slower the better, but not so slowly that you feel light-headed or uncomfortable. If that happens, pick up the pace a bit or take a break. The goal here is to relax; it's not a competition.

When you deepen your breathing, you stabilize the nervous system and improve the quality of oxygen in your body. Your body rejoices, too, because it likes it when you pay attention to it. Most of the time, we just expect our body to work the way we want it to, but we don't do much to help it along. Breath-work helps. Holding the breath in, like we do here, is helpful, too. Studies have shown that keeping in carbon dioxide longer triggers cellular repair throughout the body, so if you're sick or injured, the four-fold breath can be especially helpful. It's also helpful if you're stressed or angry, and not just because it soothes the nervous system. When you pay attention to your breath, you're not paying attention to the random thoughts and worries cycling through your head. You're too busy trying to remember to breath and counting to worry about how you did on that trig test or what Lina said to Malik in study hall. You get to just focus on you. Your body. Think of your body as your life partner. You might get married and have kids someday, but your body — that's who you want to become best friends with. You want to learn all its cues, its desires and fears. Then, you can really start to work together.

There are three more great breathing techniques that I think everyone should know: Breath of the Sun, Breath of the Moon, and Breath of Fire. These breaths are as old as, well, the sun. Yogis have been practicing them in India for centuries. Like the four-fold breath, you can do the first two in public anyone being the wiser, but you'll probably want to save Breath of Fire for home.

Breath of the Sun can be used to gently boost your physical and mental energy, activating the production of positive energy in the body and exciting cells. It's great to use when your energy levels are dropping, at the onset of illness or if you are feeling unmotivated. Extend your fingers on your left hand and use your left thumb to block off your left nostril so that you are breathing through your right nostril. Place your right hand on your right knee with thumb and forefinger making a circle and the rest of your fingers extended. Breathe slowly for 26 breaths.

Breath of the Moon helps to regulate feminine, cooling lunar energy in the body, to relax and calm yourself when you are feeling stressed or anxious. It's a good one to use at the end of the day when you're ready to go to sleep. Extend your fingers on your right hand and use your right thumb to block off your right nostril so that you are breathing through your left nostril. Place your left hand on your left knee with thumb and forefinger making a circle and the rest of your fingers extended. Breathe slowly for 26 breaths.

Both of these breaths can be performed quietly around other people without anyone noticing. Just lean your cheek on one hand to block off the proper nostril. It's not true to Ayurvedic form, but it will still have a beneficial effect. When you are looking for something that will amp you up, try this next breath instead of reaching for caffeine.

I like to say the **Breath of Fire** is like the Breath of the Sun squared. Sit straight and tall with your legs in the lotus position (crisscrossed) and breathe fast and deeply through your nose using your diaphragm, 1-3 breaths per second. This increases fire energy in the body, benefits the central nervous system, improves digestion and liver function, increases lung capacity and helps the body burn more calories. It sounds a bit like hyperventilating, but since you are performing deep breaths with the use of your diaphragm, it's very different and you should be getting all the oxygen you need; if you're not, slow down!

Keep one hand on your diaphragm so that you can monitor your form and make sure you are doing it right. If it's hard to keep your diaphragm pushing in and out so quickly, again, slow down. When you're doing it right, you'll notice your torso begin to rock forward and backward slightly with your breaths. Yogis strive to do this breath for 31 minutes a day, but just 2-3 minutes every morning will wake you up and help you strengthen core abdominal and spinal muscles. The more regularly you practice, the longer you will be able to sustain the Breath of Fire. Don't worry if you can only do it for a minute or two the first time — becoming a dragon is hard!

When you practice these breaths, it can be additionally beneficial to use one of the following mudras or hand gestures. Mudras are used in many traditions because each finger is associated with a different element and function in the body. The thumb represents ether, or spirit, without which your body would not function. The forefinger is the air finger, governing thoughts. Your middle finger is fire, for creativity, passion, and anger. The ring finger is all about water and emotions — no wonder most cultures wear their wedding rings on that finger! And, last but not least, your pinky represents the earth, our inner strength and how well we're connecting with our purpose here in this life. When you **massage your fingers or toes**, or use your hands to make mudras, you're activating and balancing the elements in your body. We'll talk more about the elements later, but for now, try some of these mudras (pictured on the following page) while you practice your breath-work.

The Bhudi mudra balances your ether and earth elements, helping you connect your body and spirit. It is often used to enhance communication, intuition and psychic abilities. Touch the tips of your thumb and pinky together and extend the three middle fingers.

The Ahamkara mudra is used to combat fear and is believed to raise self-confidence. Most westerners know it well as the "All OK" symbol. Bend your middle finger and place your thumb on its second phalanx, keeping your other three fingers held straight up.

The Kubera mudra is called the "Make a Wish" mudra. Use this mudra with any deep breathing exercise to center and align yourself to your soul purpose and desire, and then state your intentions or wishes several times out loud while you visualize their manifestation. Touch the tips of your thumb, index, and middle fingers together and tuck your ring finger and pinky your palm.

The Mukula, or Samana, mudra is used most often to instigate healing in the body. All five elements are brought together here to balance their energies and create harmony. With this mudra, energy takes form and creative energy can easily be directed to manifest with efficiency and purpose. Bring all five fingertips together and point upward for general meditation. In healing, place the fingertips of the part of the body that is needing healing or relief.

The next time you find yourself getting bored in class or stressing out at home, try the Breath of the Sun or the Four-Fold Breath. Pretty soon, you'll know what it actually means to breathe easy!

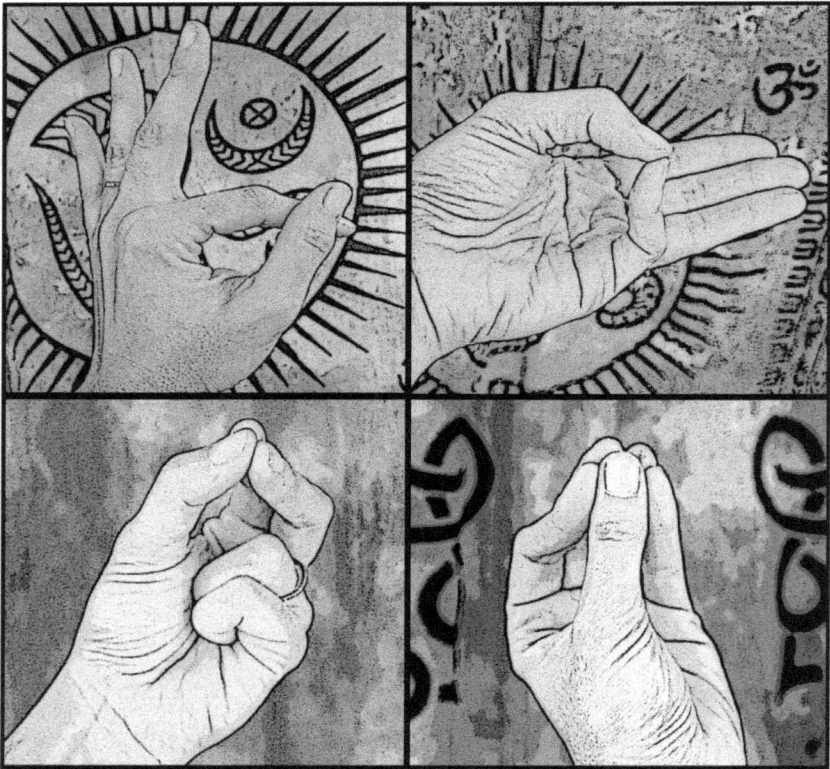

Clockwise from Top Left: Ahamkara, Bhudi, Kubera, Mukula

Songs for the Velociraptor in Your Brain

You've heard it all before. Teens are different. You're hormonal, you lack boundaries, you don't listen, blah, blah, blah. Adults act like they can't remember how hard it is to be a teen — and maybe they don't. Scientists have been diving down into the realities of the teenage brain and it turns out there's a lot more going on than anyone realized.

Teen brains aren't just different. They're getting completely rewired. Whole sections are getting upgraded, deleted, re-written. It's a complex process that transforms the child brain into an adult brain over the course of ten years and it is happening all the time. When you sleep. When you are in class. When your mother is yelling at you because you forgot (again) to put away your laundry.

The gray matter of your young brain, parts that you didn't use as a child, parts you won't need later, are slowly being deleted. The process starts in the back of your brain — where your coordination and balance are regulated — and moves through the areas pertaining to your sleep cycles, your emotions, and your visual processing. You start noticing beauty more, wanting to use your body more. You need more sleep and it's a great time to learn to drive, skate or ski. You move with more confidence because you are fully in the moment — so why don't you feel great, too?

Your memories and perceptions are stronger than ever now, along with your judgments. Your brain is deciding what information it wants to hone and keep, and this affects how you see the world. Everything feels like it's life and death — because for your brain, it is. This might not sound or feel rational, but there's not much you can do about it. Your prefrontal cortex, the part of your brain that helps you make rational, well-reasoned decisions, will be the last part of your brain to be rewired. It's also the part of your brain that helps you think through consequences and think about the future. Scientists say that while this reconstruction is going on teens rely mostly on their amygdala for making decisions: the predatory, prehistoric part of our brain that governs emotions, aggression, and impulses, the part that helped us hunt mammoths and take risks to win healthy mates.

That's right. You see where I am going here. You are discerning stimuli with a finely-tuned predator's brain, wired to match your peak physical age. But sometimes you say or do things without thinking, things you wouldn't normally do. Your internal velociraptor reacts, strikes, and defends — sometimes with the worst sort of after-effects. Shame, embarrassment, regret — some days you might wonder who's taken over your body.

It's confusing. You might say and do things you don't really mean. It's normal at any age to lash out when you feel hurt or betrayed, but as a teenager, your brain is literally programmed to act first, speak quickly, and think later. You might make bad decisions. In fact, I can pretty much guarantee that at some point you will. The important thing here, the way to grow up gracefully, is to accept the mistakes as part of your learning process. Embrace them. And, whenever possible, forgive yourself and atone as needed through kindness.

The good news here is that even as your brain is shifting itself to become a leaner, better decision-making machine, your core personality has already been established. You know who you are. You know what you like. And you do know how to communicate, even if it doesn't always feel that way. Using sound to alter and raise our vibration, we can literally shift our brain waves and our behavior.

In our normal waking states, humans operate at different states at different age ranges. This is significant because the brain learns new behavior and gathers information more easily the slower it is cycling. The brains of babies and toddlers operate almost exclusively in Delta waves. Everything is new, and everything they see, hear, touch, taste or smell becomes instantly encoded in their brain for future recall. Between the ages of four and seven years, most children are operating in Theta states. They still learn very quickly, but their brains are a bit more discerning and filter out certain information if they don't want it. Primarily in the Alpha state, older children and young teenagers require an average of twenty-one repetitions to learn new behavior. After the age of fourteen, the brain waves stay primarily in the Beta range, and adults will need a thousand repetitions or more to learn new behaviors, unless they consciously put themselves into a slower brain cycle for learning. This is why affirmations, guided meditation, and hypnosis often produce such remarkable results, allowing you to program desirable habits and behaviors within two to eight weeks. Each technique lets you repeat a message until the brain accepts that you truly want to encode this new behavior or idea into its patterns of belief.

Slower brain waves have been shown to induce greater healing ability within the body, which is part of why modern medicine uses medically-induced comas to help trauma victims heal. The deep sleep-state relieves the patient somewhat from the conscious effect of pain, while a body in Delta state will experience increased Human Growth hormone, DHEA and melatonin. These same states can greatly benefit the teen body and brain as they grow and change. Teens don't just love to sleep — your bodies and brains need it! Try to get at least nine hours a night, increasing to ten or eleven whenever possible. To boost your sleep's effectiveness, slow your waves by listening to the right music before bed.

Some music can raise our energy or help us sleep. Why is that? Music – SOUND – can change your brain waves. The brain operates at a wide spectrum of frequencies at all times, but there is always a dominant wavelength depending on what you are doing. These brain waves are measurable by EEG readings and the five main ranges are known as Beta, Alpha, Theta, Delta and Gamma waves.

Gamma waves are the fastest at 40+ Hz. They indicate a hyper-aware state of heightened perception and simultaneous thought processing. They are present during the flight or fight response, and are also found in people with better memories. Gamma waves help us see every minute detail. **Beta** waves are the dominant indicator of adult waking brain activity. They cycle 13-30 times per second and elicit logical thoughts and sense activation. **Alpha** waves register at 8 to 12 cycles per second and indicate a relaxed, intuitive mindset. It is the state most commonly sought during meditation. Studies show that students perform better and develop more interest in their studies when learning from an alpha state. **Theta** brain waves come in at 4 to 8 cycles per second and indicate deeper trance or dream states with an active unconscious. Theta and Alpha waves tend to be more prevalent in creative personalities and those with ADHD – what some call the DaVinci and Einstein types. **Delta** waves are the slowest at 0.5 to 4 cycles per second. It is the deepest form of relaxation without dreams.

Music which incorporates **monaural beats and isochronic tones** is marketed extensively online and allows the listener to easily synchronize with any brain wave state simply by putting on a CD. Robert Monroe's **binaural beats** are marketed under the name "Hemi-Sync" and benefit from decades of research at the Monroe Institute for Applied Sciences, which also happened to work with the CIA to develop multiple psychic spy programs. These recordings are also some of the most pleasant to listen to, but they do require headphones for effective listening. There are also a lot of really great YouTube videos using monaural beats and specific frequencies to help you sleep, relax, study or heal. Find some you like and let them play as you fall asleep, you just might be surprised by the results.

Repetitive chanting, singing bowls and drumming are also effective techniques used to still the mind and affect the brain. This is the key to why drumming has long been used throughout the world as a tool for entering trance states, especially for healing and grounding work.

The Voice

Your voice is not just for talking and singing. It is one of your greatest tools for self-expression. It belongs to the body, but the mind almost always controls what it is and isn't allowed to say. When a person begins to experience throat, sinus, or respiration problems, I often ask "What are you not saying or admitting? What are you holding in? What are you holding back?" But the truth is that we are always holding something back. We don't allow ourselves to whoop and holler, coo and cry, the way we did when we were young. And the power of our voice goes unheard, unused. Toning, singing, and chanting are ways to get back in touch with that, back in touch with our body, back in touch with our true selves.

Toning is simple. Start by groaning and moaning, your deepest, lowest, most primal sounds. Let them come out however they want, soft and low, loud and hard, for as long as they want. The voice, at some point, will begin to naturally rise, to naturally soften. A sigh is often heard at this point – the time when the voice gives into to its joy at having been released, at having permission to express itself. It might begin to chant particular sounds, it might begin to hold a higher-pitched tone, just let it come. The lower tones are a release, they let go of old energy. The higher tones begin to bring healing, they bless and restore, they activate and align. They are, literally, higher vibrations. Pay attention to your body while you tone, see where the different sounds resonate, what makes you feel more energized, what feels uncomfortable or strange. Toning helps break through blockages in the body – pay attention to the area and the related chakra to see what sort of emotional issues or old patterns you might be clearing out (ie: the lungs might relate to grief or anger, legs to support or feeling stuck, pelvis to survival issues or sexuality)

Toning can be used to heal over long distances (sound waves go on forever) or in person. It can be used to charge and activate items for holy, sacred usage. It can be used to raise your vibration. Many people, once they start toning, do it every day. The shower or the car are great places for this. You can tone or chant the syllables on the following page, or try longer phrases that invoke compassion, higher spirits, or positive feelings such as "All is well" or "Om Nimah Shivaya." **Chanting** works to balance the hormones, immune system and nervous system. When you chant, your tongue presses against the top of your mouth, or palate, in a variety of ways. This action stimulates glands that communicate with the pituitary, hypothalamus, and thalamus. Traditionally, chants are often repeated 108 times, but you can go with whatever number works for you.

Spiritual Syllables

AH – Believed by the majority of spiritual systems, including Tibetan Buddhism and Hebrew Kabbalah, to be the first sound, the word that created the world. It invokes the seed of Spirit and creation. The Ah in amen, literally invoking the idea "So Be It." It is a compassionate, comforting sound connected to the heart chakra. It is the first sound we make when we are born as we breathe in, and the sound we make on our last, final breath.

OM or AUM – In Sanskrit, this is the sound of Spirit, the sound that birthed the universe. It is the first primordial vibration, the sound of creation and birth. It resonates within the diaphragm and solar plexus.

HU, YOU or OO - Another seed sound believed by the Sufis and various yoga traditions to be the sound of creation. Chanting this sound is believed to lead to enlightenment and ascension. It can connect well to both the throat chakra and the root chakra.

EE – Energizing and awakening. It opens the third eye chakra and cleanses the pineal gland.

The Uncaged Voice

The first step to living the life you want is getting comfortable with your own voice and expressing your own needs. So get used to it. Spend the next month toning every day for a few minutes. At the start of the day, some toning will help you get energized and focused. At the end of the day, toning can help you release stress and heal bruised feelings. Try both and see what works best for you. Singing, too, is a great exercise and a way to reach for your best feelings. Pay attention to your moods and the music you listen to. Sometimes, our favorite songs sound like a lot of fun but the lyrics are actually not that positive. You might not realize it, but your brain is listening closely to that verse about being all alone and afraid and internalizing the message. If you've been feeling nervous or angry a lot lately, try listening to songs that have more positive messages and see how your mood shifts. Sometimes it's the opposite: a song might have great lyrics, but the frequency of the music is agitating your nervous system. Experiment with different artists and genres throughout the week and see what makes you feel good. And of course, use that voice! Belting out a song about being fearless can really boost your confidence the night before a big test. Your brain is always constantly taking cues about how you want to feel from the things you surround yourself with and what you pay attention to. If you watch horror movies all the time, part of your brain will begin looking for aspects of situations that will scare you, because it will think that you prefer being in a heightened state of stress.

There are many ways to program and condition the mind: how are you programming yours?

Try singing and toning daily and see how your experience and emotions shift. Use your voice to release the feelings you don't want to carry around anymore. If you feel like you don't have anywhere you feel comfortable singing or toning, think about that, too. Everybody needs space where they can just be themselves. What are some steps you can take to find yours? Can you join a chorus at school or in a local church? Can you play music in the shower and sing there? Start small if you have to, hum under your breath while you fall asleep of blow dry your hair. As you become more and more comfortable giving your voice the freedom it craves, you will begin to feel more centered and you will begin to communicate your own personal truth more clearly.

What does that mean? Turn the page and check out the next chapter, where we'll talk about open communication and what that can look like.

Opening Doors with Open Communication

When we communicate clearly and openly, it is easier for the world around us to respond the way we want it to. Think about it. If we don't make a wishlist or tell our family about the new Tombraider game that just came out, how will anyone know which game to buy you for your birthday? You might not always get what you want in life, but if you don't express your preferences and desires, if the universe doesn't know what makes you happy, then how can the universe conspire to please you? The first step to living a satisfying life is identifying who you really are — what excites you, what are your values, and how would a life centered around those things really look? The clearer we get about who we are and what makes us tick, the more open we are with ourselves, the easier it becomes to deal with the outside world. Not just your friends, but your family, teachers and eventually, your co-workers, employees, and bosses. When you know who you are and how your own emotions work, you can stay calmer in arguments and identify the best paths towards your goals.

In the previous chapter, we talked about forgiving yourself for saying or doing things you don't really mean. Unless you plan on living on a mountaintop in a cave, you're going to need to learn to get along with other people and negotiate difficult conversations. Throughout your teen years and well beyond, you will find yourself in situations where it isn't easy to get along with the people around you. Teachers can be difficult. Parents might sound harsh. Group projects might not go smoothly.

We can't always choose who we get to work with in life, but we do get to choose how we work with them.

Let's start with the adults in our lives and our friends. Sometimes, you might find yourself wondering if anyone truly cares about you. Mom took away your internet because you swore at dinner. Your foster dad scolded you for not turning in your homework. Your friend stormed away when you cracked a silly joke.

The people who love us the most also hurt us the most when they take that love away. But is that what they're really doing? Most parents and caregivers just want kids to be happy, safe and healthy — that's what most people adults mean when they say they want the best for you. For the first decade of your life, they got to choose how that would happen. Now, they have to share that responsibility with you and it's difficult. They might not always agree with your choices, and this can cause friction. Mom might think the best way for you to be happy is to conduct yourself with good manners, so you can get a good job and a nice spouse. You believe freedom of expression is a core right, and you plan to use that right daily as a writer. Who is she to stifle your voice? Your foster parent believes you need to pass algebra so you can become a scientist, something he thinks you'd be great at. You'd rather use your problem-solving skills to crack criminal cases and make neighborhoods like yours safer. Your friend is concerned about his sister who is having a hard time learning to read; when you made fun of your teacher droning through the history lesson, it reminded him of his own worries.

Sometimes, when people get upset with us, it's because they're worried about you or something else. Before you get angry another person, try to look at things from their perspective. Why are they really upset with you? Chances are, the reasons go deeper than you think. There is a saying that everyone you talk with is just a mirror of yourself. In a way, it's true. Our feelings about other's behavior often reflect our fears and concerns about ourselves, triggering strong reactions in return: revulsion, anger, disappointment. We'll dig deep into this concept and how to get over those triggers in the Chapter "What's Your Damage." First, though, we need to explore the concepts of empathy, compassion, and open communication.

Have you ever heard the saying, "Before you judge someone, walk a mile in their shoes"? Everyone has their own problems. A lot of times, when someone is acting rude or angry it has nothing to do with you and everything to do with themselves. When your foster dad sees you failing algebra, it makes him worried because he wants you to have lots of career choices.

That's what he'll say anyway, to himself and you. Really, if he was to dig a little further into his belief systems, he'd probably find that what's upsetting him goes much deeper. He's worried that if you work as a cop, you might get hurt. Not only could you lose your ability to make money and buy groceries, you could lose your life. He's trying not to think about all the dangers you might face when you grow up, and when you brought back that D- last week that became harder. Scarier. Your friend who got mad because you made fun of the teacher? They're worried about their sister failing her class and being made fun of. And even deeper in their heart, they worry you might start making fun of them, too, if they ever tell a boring story. That's why they haven't talked to you about their sister. They're not sure they can really trust you, and that hurts. It always hurts when we're not sure we're making a good connection.

Does that mean that you should let your friends or adults get away with behaving badly? Of course not. But if we can imagine how the other person might be feeling then we have a better chance to improve the relationship and resolve and conflicts. When you don't like how things are going with another person, take a deep breath and ask yourself **"How would I feel if it were me...?"**

It might be hard to imagine yourself as a parent or teacher, but the truth is everyone in their life is a teacher to someone, including you. Everyone we meet has the potential to show us something new about the world or ourselves. You never know where your most important life lessons might come from, how a chance encounter might completely change your mind about something. Dialogue is important, even if it's just with ourselves. In fact, sometimes that's the best conversation we can have. Remember Mom, who wants you to have better manners and get a steady job? After you've both cooled off, why not sit down with her ask her straight up: "Why do you always try to steer me away from being a writer? I thought you liked my short stories?" The question will probably surprise her, because she does like your stories. They enchant her, and she thinks you're brilliant. But, she also knows that being a writer can be difficult, and she wants to see you happy. Will other people think you're brilliant, too? What if you can't support yourself being a writer? We've all heard the sayings about starving artists. When she hears you swearing or talking balk to her, it upsets her because a part of her knows you might not share those same concerns. Pretty soon you'll be leaving home and you're not going to make the same choices she would — choices she thinks are safer, easier. At least, if you know how to be polite, you might make a great impression on someone — a publisher or mentor — who could help you one day.

She might not be able to tell you things, but then again, she might. If you don't keep the lines of communication open, you'll never have the chance to find out. Remember that good talks don't have to be long or scary. Even a couple of sentences back and forth can go a long way towards improving relationships with someone. The key is to try to approach things with clarity and an open mind. Try not to start a conversation angry. Take a minute (or a day) to think about what exactly you want to say. Write down a few opening lines. The best questions are open-ended and unbiased. Name the problem and what you want to happen. Did your science partner lock you out of a shared computer document so you couldn't input your work? Instead of getting offended and feeling targeted, try to remember that they might not have done it on purpose. Say: "I'm locked out. Can you let me back in?" Make sure they can hear and understand you — eye contact is a good indicator that they do. If they don't do it, remember, you should never allow people to treat you badly. Tell the teacher or a counselor.

This is especially important if you are being bullied, hurt or abused in any way. If the teacher does not seem sufficiently helpful or concerned, see the school counselor. If they do not help, talk to the adults at home or another teacher or principal at the school. You have the right to feel safe and heard at school and at home: if you are surrounded by a system that does not support you, find someone who does — whether that is the superintendent, the local news, the board of education, your doctor or another friend's parent. I know that sometimes it can feel like nobody gets you, but that's why open communication is so important. It's hard to read a book when the cover is shut. The same goes for people. No one can know what you're thinking, what you're going through, unless you tell them. Actions speak loudly, too. When you slam the door to your bedroom when you get home from school, you're announcing to the adults at home that you're unhappy. Don't be surprised, then, when they come into your room and ask you "What's wrong with you? Why are you slamming doors?" They might seem mad, too. Instead of yelling for them to get out of your room, imagine for a moment how you might feel if they came into your room while you were playing a video game, didn't say hi, and then stormed out and slammed the door. You might think that you had done something to upset them, or you might just be angry that they had messed up your progress on a boss level. Take a deep breath, ask yourself "If it were me..." and then consider telling them a little bit about what's going on. Maybe it's too embarrassing, or you just don't want to talk. That's okay, too. You should have the right to choose where and what you discuss. Let them know it's been a rough day and you're not ready to talk about it. If you can speak openly with other people, you may be surprised to find that they begin to trust you more, too. Pretty soon, you'll be on your way to a life with less drama and more inner peace, because you won't be engaging with the games people play when they're trying to figure you out.

Be honest, be open, and the world will be more open with you. Does that mean that you won't ever have arguments or problems with other people? Of course not. But if you can act impeccably, if you strive for open communication and well-intentioned behavior in every situation, you will always have the pleasure of knowing that whatever is happening is not about you: it's about them. You'll know that the drama isn't yours, it's theirs. Once you assign ownership of a drama to its true source, you can let go of all the unpleasant feelings that go with it. We'll talk more about empathy, drama, and compassion in the chapter "Empath Problems." First, though, let's see if we can figure out more about what really bothers you, and why.

What's Your Damage?

Everybody gets angry and sad sometimes. It's normal. There's a lot of pressure on us to stay happy and "normal" all the time, but it's not always realistic or even healthy. Most cultural traditions have stories that teach us to stay ever in the light. Cautionary tales like **Little Red Riding Hood**, **Goldilocks, and Dracula.** We are taught from early ages that straying into the dark areas of the wood, leaving the well-worn, well-lit paths, will lead us into danger. These stories are well-meant, but it is important to explore the darker side of things, too, so that we can truly understand what is light, and what is dark. Often, what we believe to be dark is actually supporting and nourishing us in ways we never imagined.

We all have aspects of ourselves that we don't embrace. Behaviors we are less than proud of, habits that we would like to change. We also have parts of ourselves that we love, ways that we act that we think are exemplary, things we do that put us above reproach or make us better people. Carl Jung explained that our shadow self is "that which we think we are not." Our shadow self encourages all of us to do things that aren't so great: look at someone and cringe at their outfit; mock another person for something they believe in; believe that we are better (or worse) than someone else. A lot of pain in life stems from these kinds of judgments.

So why do we do it?

Sometimes, putting other people down can feel good — it makes us feel like we are winning. What most people don't realize is that *all* the judgments we make harm us more in the long run than anything else we could do to ourselves.

Every judgment you make stems from a belief you have about yourself in relation to the world outside of you. This means each time you judge someone or something, you also judge yourself. Judgment arises when we overlay external energies and systems of belief over our own. Yet your soul, your truest aspect of self that is one with Spirit, knows better. It knows you are one with everything, that there can be no aspect of reality separate from your self, so every judgment creates a rift between you and Source. This is the origin of the "dark" that sets itself aside from the light. At ALL moments, in all aspects, the dark is actually one and the same as the light. It can never separate itself. But darkness judges itself separate, and so experiences reality as something external from itself, removed from itself. At best, judgment can lead to depression and apathy; at its worst, judgment leads individuals and society to support social inequities, systems of abuse, suicide, and violence.

Once, I had a conversation with a client about the problems judgment had created throughout her childhood and later in her career. She had always competed with her sister. When she was happy, her sister was sad. While she worked hard for good grades, her sister partied like a rock star and suffered at the hands of bullies. Her whole life, she fought to prove that she was nothing like her sister, that she was good, kind, successful.

Her sister was miserable. And, even though she put on a happy face, my client was also miserable. And it didn't stop there. The same sort of dramas followed her throughout her career and marriage, with everyone being annoyed that she made them look bad, that she overachieved, hit every deadline, befriended every client. She was often accused of being fake, since "no one can possibly be happy all the time." Finally, frustrated with herself for allowing her boss's comments to get under her skin, she pleaded with me.

"Do you have any idea how hard it is to be this intelligent and not judge other people?"

And so we entered into a discussion of discernment versus judgment. When you assign value to differences, you are no longer noting or perceiving a dichotomy, you are rendering a judgment. I explained the difference between knowing you don't like a book or politician, and condemning another person for their enjoyment of what you do not like. The first is an internal process or evaluation wherein you discern your inner (soul) preferences. The second lays down an external hologram of judgment over the object or situation. In real-world terms, in the first instance, you've marked an answer incorrect on a quiz; in the second, you've taken twenty points off the final grade or decided to debate the validity of a different answer.

As my client and I sat with each other, we came to understand just how game-changing it could be for both her mental and emotional well-being to refrain from judgment and strive for non-duality. This was a word she had never heard of before.

Non-duality is a philosophy that teaches us that nothing is separate: good and bad are one, light and dark is one, sadness and happiness are one, and all experiences are equal. Joy is not better than sadness. Suffering comes because we judge our situation as lacking in some way. When we embrace non-duality, we can release anxiety and fear. Life becomes smoother, as happiness is no longer the goal, but simply being present and open at all times.

This does not mean, of course, that we do not laugh and play and experience joy. It simply means that we relax our expectations a bit and continue to behave diligently and honorably for the sheer power of the moment. For being alive. For being part of Source. We become warriors, acting impeccably whether we are sweeping floors, doing homework, trying on dresses with friends, or playing a video game. We become fully invested in every minute, every day. Not to win. Not to prove something. To live fully, as much as we can, as well as we can, while we can. We can stop over-thinking things and worrying about the external world so much, and focus more on the small miracle of every second we have in this body.

Of course, sometimes it's easier said than done. Just because you stop judging people and situations, doesn't mean everyone else around you will, too. It's hard work being human! If you're going to live in a busy world, interacting with other beings that may have totally different goals and values than you, you're probably going to come out with some emotional bumps and bruises. A Buddhist leader and holy man, the Dalai Lama himself is still angry with the Chinese government for how it has treated the people of Tibet and his fellow monks. He admits some days are harder than others, but takes joy in knowing that his life is a work in progress.

At the end of the day, that's all of us can do: take each day as it comes and strive for balance. Life is a mirror, what we judge, judges us. And when we are in balance, the world around us can rise more easily to meet us.

There are some fun things you can do to help you release judgment, too. Here, I am going to include three of my favorite exercises. The first will help you to appreciate the very same qualities you dislike most and the second will help you uncover the reason you really hate these things in the first place.

To start, let's get back to that first thing I mentioned, the idea that darkness is evil. God energy is manifested at its highest and truest vibration as light. Lower vibrations of Source energy appear "dark", but they are also Source energy. After all, God, Chi, Source — that energy is everywhere, at all times, in all things. It is never missing. It is never gone. It can't be turned off or excluded from any part or any reality. This is a defining characteristic of Source.

So then, what defines a vibration as high or low, light or dark? Any being or thing that feels excluded from Source or resists its connection to Source energy lowers its vibration. The more connected one feels to Source, the lighter one's vibration seems and the "lighter" one is. Now, is that person truly more a part of Source than someone else who is trying to turn away from Source energy? No. It's impossible to not be part of Source. You are always part of Source, regardless of what you feel, do or believe. But your thoughts and beliefs create your vibrational status, so the more connected you think you are, the lighter you will feel and become. Conversely, the more disconnected you feel, the darker the shadow you create as you turn away from Source. This shadow can be cast onto the world around you, lowering the vibration of everything and everyone around you, much like a tree will cast a shadow over a picnic as the sun sets.

Becoming light and raising your vibration is simply a matter of embracing Source energy. All you need to do is invite it into your light with an open heart and mind. The more you resist this light, the more you will feel down and dark. If you are angry, anxious or depressed, that is a good indicator that you are not aligning with Source energy. **Connecting to Source always feels good.** Being on your true path and remaining open to the possibilities of creation will always bring joy to yourself and the people around you.

A good way to evaluate where you are at is to check your reactions to other people. How you feel around certain people can show you what you value in yourself, and what you are wanting to deny or reject. Here is an example: You hold the belief that lying is bad and if someone lies to you, you will become very angry and upset. These emotions are a sign that you need to take a moment and get back into the flow of the Universal Source Energy. Most likely you developed your feelings about deceit when you were punished as a child for lying. You decided right then that you did not want to be "bad", you did not want to be punished, and so you did your best never to lie again. But you were not bad. You cannot be bad. You are Source. So this was a false teaching.

You must rise above judgments and a black and white belief system. Source does not judge itself. It embraces all aspects of itself, nurturing the dark into the light, always striving to raise vibration without punitive measures. Some lies are good. Sometimes people are not ready to hear the full truth. The same parents who teach their children to never, ever lie, also lie all the time to those children, sometimes out of convenience, sometimes to protect them, sometimes to create more magic or mystery in their child's life (The Tooth Fairy).

Much of our most positive behaviors arise out of the Dark. We do not like to be hit or made fun of, so we teach our children that bullying and hitting is wrong. We do not like when people will not share with us, and so we are careful to be generous with others. We fear being homeless, so we donate items and money to shelters for people and animals. True compassion derives from empathy, the ability to put oneself in another person's shoes and feel what they feel. This is why it is so important to release a judgmental mindset. You cannot truly feel what another person feels if you are judging them to be below you or evil. Judgment creates darkness as it tries to block out the light. There is light in all beings, in all things. Source is everywhere. No one is truly evil. No one is truly bad. Buddha taught that if you truly loved yourself, you could never hurt another being. We come back to the Buddhist teaching of non-duality with the idea that to be fully enlightened one must first let go of beliefs and judgments based in duality – light/dark, worthy/unworthy, good/bad. To judge someone as bad means that you are also judging Source to be bad, and since you are Source, then you are judging yourself to be bad. Buddhists believe this cycle is the birthplace of all negative emotion, all apathy and depression, and I think they're onto something, too.

When we spend time digging out our darkest aspects, we can bring them into the light. You can see what limiting beliefs you might have that are holding you back, if you have any judgments that regularly lower your vibration and keep you unhappy, and how some of your "dark" aspects actually help make you stronger or better. Once you do this, you embrace your whole self, with your whole heart. Once something is identified, it can't stay hidden. Dark pieces brought into the light through identification are immediately illuminated by this simple act.

You are not bad. You cannot be bad. Let in the light, and allow your emotions to rise.

When you allow the light to shine on your darkest pieces, you can begin to see the good in everyone and release negative patterns of judgment that have been sabotaging your work or your personal life. Relationships will begin to flow more easily. Guilt, shame, and anger can be replaced with forgiveness, acceptance and compassion.

It's All Part of You

Here's an exercise you can do to help you come to terms with the outside world.

1. Write down the names of three people who inspire you. These can be YouTube stars or people you know. Next to each person, write down a positive trait that you admire about them (ie: Beyoncé/Creativity, That Girl in Science Class/Organization, Your Best Friend/Fearlessness).

2. Take a minute to reflect on the fact that all of these traits are also inside you, or else you would not be capable of admiring them. *Read that again.* If you weren't already a creative person, you would not be able to appreciate another person's creativity. Everything you love, is already inside you.

3. Next, write down the opposite of each trait, its dark side. (ie: Beyoncé/People Pleaser, That Girl in Science/Anxiety, Your Best Friend/Intimidating).

4. Now, take some time to recognize that sometimes you can act that way, too. You also have these characteristics inside you.

5. Finally, have a conversation with these dark shadow traits. Ask each one how it benefits, serves or teaches you. *(ie: People-*

pleasing encourages me stay helpful, even when I'd rather take the easy way out. It helps me to navigate social situations. When I am anxious, I can channel the energy into positive actions, helping move me through whatever I am experiencing. When I need to be strong and stand up for myself, I can draw on my intimidating side for protection.) Accept these shadow traits for the gifts they are, and think about how you can consciously incorporate them into your life in positive ways.

You can also reverse the exercise, starting with the name of someone you are having trouble with and writing down a few negative traits that this person has. Write down the first words that come to you. Recognize that you also have these traits and that you are trying to disown them in yourself. Thinking about each trait, where do you feel it in your body? Send light and love to each area, visualize it glowing brightly and imagine you are giving yourself a nice, long hug. If you want, you can even wrap your arms around yourself — studies have shown that hugging yourself releases endorphins in the body and soothes nerves! Ask how you can turn these traits around in yourself so that they can serve you. Then write down the opposite of each trait, the positive quality. Read the list over, really sounding out each word and smile knowing that you also have these good qualities. Feel how they make your heart light up.

Deactivating Buttons & Triggers

Buttons and triggers are judgment based beliefs held deep within the psyche that affect the way you think, feel and do at a subconscious level, like the judgments we discussed in the previous section. The best way to identify triggers is by finding something that bothers you regularly, say when someone dog-ears a borrowed book or double dips in your salsa.

Once you have identified one of your buttons, you will see that this deep-held belief can trigger you in a variety of situations. When something bothers you, take a few moments to try and **trace the trigger** back to the beginning. Let's use the example of the dog-eared book. Ask yourself, why is it bothering you? *Dog-earing books is disrespectful. It damages the paper.* Why does this matter? *That book cost money. I can't just go out and get a new one. I saved a long time to get that book.* So what? *Well, money is hard to come by. What if I can't get more? Doesn't he realize how hard I worked to buy that book?*

Right there, in just a few short sentences, we've gotten to the root of the problem. Two roots, actually, in this case. On one hand, you feel undervalued and like your boundaries are being disrespected. On the other hand, you are stuck in survival mode, worrying about money and abundance. Now that you know what is really bothering you, you can focus on deactivating those buttons.

Take a moment to fully *feel* each emotional trigger in your body. Dive deep into the self-limiting belief or emotion. Let it fill you up so you can fully feel it: all the anger, sadness, blame, whatever the emotions are that come along with this belief. Feel it and acknowledge the feeling. Using our example, we might focus on feelings of lack and being undervalued. Tell yourself **"I made this feeling of _____. I am the power and the light of the universe, I am all of Source, and I made this feeling. I created this belief. It does not own me. I own it. It has no power over me."** Embrace the feeling. It is not wrong or bad. It simply is. Notice the parts of your body where this belief resides, where you feel heavy or uncomfortable. These are areas that might benefit from further energy work or nurturing after the initial session is done. Bring all your light and power into this part of your body, see the light flowing through your crown chakra, flooding through your body and emanating from this space. Remember that you are the light.

Remember that older teens might need to practice something over 100 times in order to make it a true belief – affirmations and the Emotional Freedom Technique below are particularly well-suited for this sort of repetitive work.

The Emotional Freedom Technique

It's a great name, isn't it? Wouldn't you like to be free from the limits of your beliefs and moods? The Emotional Freedom Technique (EFT) involves tapping on meridian points, which are like mini gateways connecting the energetic rivers that flow through your entire body. These points of energy on the body are where stagnant emotions often come to rest and become trapped. Tapping on the points helps them "wake up" or activate, so that they can more easily release emotions or energetic blockages. When you combine the tapping with affirmations, the tapping helps you to remain more aware of how the body reacts to the words that the mind is forcing it to say. Good body sensations are noticed. Bad sensations are noticed. This gets you in tune with the body as it is meant to be used: as a guide and friend that helps the mind receive guidance from the soul. When the mind is NOT in tune with the soul, or when your words are out of alignment with your desires, then you will feel physical comfort. Pay attention to your body, and seek words and emotions that make you feel great in your body -- then you can flow with life more easily.

EFT is a very good tool for making your body feel appreciated while helping your affirmations penetrate all levels: spirit, mental, physical. EFT brings your body into agreement with your ego and your subconscious while you tap on specific meridian points and you state your affirmations. EFT can involve both positive and negative affirmations, using negative affirmations to reprogram the body towards the positive. The key is for your positive affirmations to be as upbeat as possible. The positive always outweighs the negative. Do not forget to reach for joy while you are tapping!

Below, I outline an EFT example, but I also suggest you check out the internet. There are a lot of great EFT instructional videos on YouTube – I find this the best way to learn EFT.

How to do an EFT Treatment

While using the four fingers on your dominant hand (the hand you like to write with) to tap on the karate chop point of your other hand (the side of your palm which your pinkie connects to) say the following three times, stating your physical or emotional pain as specifically as possible:

"Even though I feel _____, I completely love and accept myself."

This statement is called the "set-up" because it sets your intention for the session. Next, tap on each of the following points in order, while saying a positive statement or simply "I love and accept myself":

- Top of the Head/Crown
- Inside of Eyebrow
- Side of eye
- Under eye on the cheek bone
- Under nose on the philtrum
- Under your lip above your chin
- Collarbone
- Under the underarm
- Back to top of head

Here is an example: Perhaps you've been feeling angry when you think about a friend at school. You could begin with the statement "Even though I am frustrated and angry with Pat, I completely love and accept myself" while you tap on your karate chop point.

Next, you'd tap on each of the following points moving down the body reaching for more and more positivity with each statement to re-program your beliefs and expectations about the situation:

- Crown Chakra/Top of the Head, "I love and accept myself."
- Inside of Eyebrow, "I am comfortable at school."
- Side of eye, "I like my classmates."
- Under eye on the cheek bone, "I remember the good times Emma and I have had."
- Under nose on the philtrum, "I enjoy all my time at school."
- Under your lip above your chin, "It is fun finding new ways to agree and solve problems."
- Collarbone, "I feel at ease and go with the flow at school."
- Under the underarm, "I enjoy talking to new people."
- Back to top of head. "I love and accept myself."

EFT works best when repeated often throughout the day. Get creative, and have fun with it. It might feel like a stretch to be positive about things in the beginning, but consistent use of EFT and shadow work will soon shift your perspective, helping you feel better about each new day.

The Mighty Pen

In this chapter, we're going to examine three ways to use the written word to clarify your thoughts and optimize your life. Philosophers and writers often say that the pen is mightier than the sword, an idea originating from the ability of well-chosen words to cut through lies, undermine propaganda, and disempower a ruler more effectively than any form of violence. Words have the power to reveal, heal, deceive and flay. The pen can be a powerful ally, not just for changing the world but in getting to know yourself. Maybe you're feeling confused, lonely, or bored. Maybe you're stuck on an idea and don't know where to start, or maybe you have too many ideas and can't quite sort them. Let's explore the first way you can use writing that is sure to help.

If you've taken a creative writing class at school, you might already be familiar with the concept of **freewriting**. Many teachers like to introduce their students to this method because it can help you break through writer's block and let your natural voice come through. I like freewriting because it allows you to get in touch with your subconscious and unleashes your will to create through self-expression. Even better, it's easy. Anyone can do it, all you need is something to write with. I find a pen and paper works best but if you prefer typing go ahead and use a computer or tablet.

Let's start.

Find yourself some paper and a pen or grab your laptop, settle down in a place you won't be disturbed, close your eyes and take a few deep breaths to clear your mind and body. Next, write down the first words that float through your mind. Don't judge them, don't think. Just write what you hear. Some people call this practice "stream of consciousness writing" because that's exactly what it is. Wherever your thoughts lead, that's what you write down. You ride the stream wherever it leads. In the beginning, the words might sound like gibberish. You might just write the same phrase or word over and over, then see phrases that make no sense. Don't worry about interpret the words as you go, just let the words out. Freewriting is a great way to practice non-judgment. Try not to read the words as you write them; you can read through what you have written when you're finished. You can set a timer for a specific amount of time, say five minutes, and stop when the timer goes off; or you can free write until your thoughts peter out or you get bored.

Chase the words with your pen while your mind self-calibrates and gets used to being given free rein. Follow the flow. Like your voice, which has been controlled for so many years, your thoughts are constantly patrolled by the ego. Words are judged to be right or wrong, cool or obsolete. Thoughts are discarded, prized, or punished based on whether they make us feel good and support the ego — the conscious system of judgment we use to navigate the physical world and survive. But what if we allowed ourselves to do more than just survive? What if we allow our soul's perspective to shine through? As your mind and body align, as the ego and soul come into calibration, the words on the paper may begin to make more and more sense. You might even find yourself getting some deep messages or working through some practical problems. And if you don't? It doesn't matter. The quality of your stream of consciousness doesn't matter. No matter what it looks like, you will have sifted through a lot of the chatter that is going on in your mind, white noise your waking brain has to work hard to ignore any time you ask it to do some problem-solving. Now, the signal is clear and you focus more easily. The brain can hear itself think. It can hear what your soul is trying to say.

Freewriting can help you make decisions more easily, focus on your science homework, or just decompress after a long day at school. The more you use it, the clearer your thoughts will be. That teen brain we talked about, the velociraptor knocking at the door? He'll be a lot quieter now that you've given him a safe space to run around in and make some noise. Try practicing free-writing every day for a few weeks and see how your inner narrative changes. I like to keep all my streams of consciousness in one place. You might want to have a special pen and pretty journal for your freewriting, or a dedicated google-doc that you add to every day. A 99-cent composition notebook and chewed up pencil are perfectly useful, too. The key is the practice, so whatever is most appealing and accessible to you will work best.

Once you've gotten used to freewriting, you can try your hand at **automatic writing**. Automatic writing has its roots in freewriting, so you'll start the same way: deep breaths, quieting the mind, and a little stream of consciousness to clear the static noise. Once you're in the flow, you can allow your ego to dialogue with your higher self by writing down a question and letting your soul answer. Before you ask though, make sure you tune your frequency a little more. Out loud, state who or what you want to get your answers from. Say something like, "Only my soul is allowed to communicate through me and these words today." Some of the most reliable and safe places to get your answers from are, in descending order: Source/God/Spirit; Your Soul (aka your higher self or spark-of-god-self); Archangels, Ascended Masters, Gods & Goddesses; Spirit Guides; Ancestors. The more removed a messenger is from Source, the less light it is likely to contain, resulting in lower vibrational messages and guidance. On the other hand, why would you want to get answers from someone who isn't an expert? If you're looking for advice about creation and manifesting, Source might be your best bet but for concrete guidance on how to organize your business, you might want to consult your soul about the best path forward or interview Aunt Pearl who died a rich, self-made woman. In that case, you might say something like "Only the highest wisdom for my greatest good may come through me today from Source and my Great-Aunt Pearl."

Your set-up statement tunes the channel and focuses your intention so that you can get the best results. Now, you just need to ask a question. Write down what you want to know. Be as clear as possible — good questions make for better answers. Then, allow the answers to come through the same way you allow yourself to free write. The only difference here is that the messages now will be coming less from your subconscious brain and more from your stated source. Some people call this type of automatic writing channeling, since you've focused yourself to tune in to a new channel with new information — new music, new noise. Others call it downloading, since the process can feel a lot like receiving an information packet from the internet. Whatever you want to call it, it's great! Write down everything you hear or think until the flow of words stops, then ask another question. Don't judge the words that come through but feel free to ask for clarification whenever you need to. Keep going until you run out of questions or the source of information says goodbye and signs off for the day. If the latter happens, you might choose to connect to another guide (Maybe Uncle Benny who owned an ice cream shop?) or stop for the day, too. Once you are done, read over the new information you received and take some time to think it over. How can you use this new information to follow your dreams? Did your guides give you steps here that you can take right now to enact a better reality? You don't have to listen to everything your higher self says, but I find when I walk hand-in-hand with Source, life unfolds pretty beautifully.

Still, physical reality can be tough to get a handle on, especially when it comes to getting organized. This is where our third journal practice comes in. If you didn't like the last two exercises, don't worry — this one is less about writing and more about finding clarity and staying focused. Invented by Ryder Carroll, a digital designer in Brooklyn, NY who wanted to keep his projects organized, the **Bullet Journal**® is a project managing, habit tracking, and goal manifesting tool for anyone can use. Scared? Don't be. Bujos, as they have been affectionately nicknamed, are amazing customizable tools that anyone can use. The harder it is for you to organize your thoughts, the more you can benefit from a Bullet Journal® — Ryder Carroll came up with the method to help himself overcome some of the difficulties posed by his learning disabilities. Named after the ever-popular organizational tool, the bullet list, these things can help you fly through tasks and hit projected targets with ease. Sound good? Let's see how they work.

If you go online you'll find hundreds of resources for bullet journaling. Fancy notebooks with dot-grid paper. Beautiful marker sets. Pinterest boards. Instagrammers and bloggers. Carroll's own mailing list and instructional guide at www.bulletjournal.com. Stencil sets, stickers and stamps. Like scrapbooking, the world of bullet journaling is vast and varied. Personally, I like to use a hard-bound sketchbook with thick, unlined paper that doesn't allow my markers to bleed through. A composition notebook can work just as well here. You'll also probably want a pencil, a fine-tipped black pen or marker, and a set of colored markers or pens with at least four colors. I'm an artist and I like bright colors, so I use a set of 48 artist-quality markers. A ruler can be helpful, too. Bujos are generally used for a few minutes every day, so keeping everything together in one spot keeps things convenient.

Once you've gathered your tools, there are a few things you'll need to do to start off right. Many people begin a new journal each year and decorate the first page of the journal with the date, the year, or an inspirational message that expresses the theme of the year, something like "Be a Unicorn!" or "Achieve & Believe!" Next, number each page of your bujo in one corner, leaving the last several pages of the notebook unnumbered. This might seem time-consuming, but trust me, it's worth it. When you've finished, turn to the last page of your bujo and write "Table of Contents" or "Index." Now, each time you create a new section or entry within the journal, you will note the page and title in your Table of Contents (TOC for short.) Carroll originally designed his system so that the TOC resides on the first four pages in the front of the journal, like a regular book, but I find it simpler to allow the sections (often called collections in bujo-speak) to flow forward from the beginning while the index works its way backward. This way, I never have to worry about running out of space in my TOC and the two parts always meet seamlessly in the end.

Once you've numbered your pages and set aside the space for your index, you get to decide what to put into your bujo.

Ultimately, a Bullet Journal® is just a tool for manifesting your best life. It's all about you, so make it yours! Have fun with it!

What kinds of things can you do in your bullet journal? Many people like to create a page each week that works like a calendar, marking important deadlines and goals. Some people draw little illustrations of the things they'd like to achieve that month, or create a habit tracker, a chart that records what goals you hit each day. Trying to get in shape? You can have a tracker for the different exercises you do each day, or check off the days you ate fresh veggies and high-quality protein. Most people's goals change over time, so you can make a new tracker each month, too. Over the summer kept track of when I hiked, swam, ate fresh, practiced the banjo, wrote a chapter, did some yoga, or had fun with my kids.

This month the kids are back in school and ski season is getting close, so I'm focusing more on work (writing and marketing) and doing some physical therapy to prepare my knees for the slopes. Trackers can be graphic and artsy or straightforward tables; here's one that I set up in chart format:

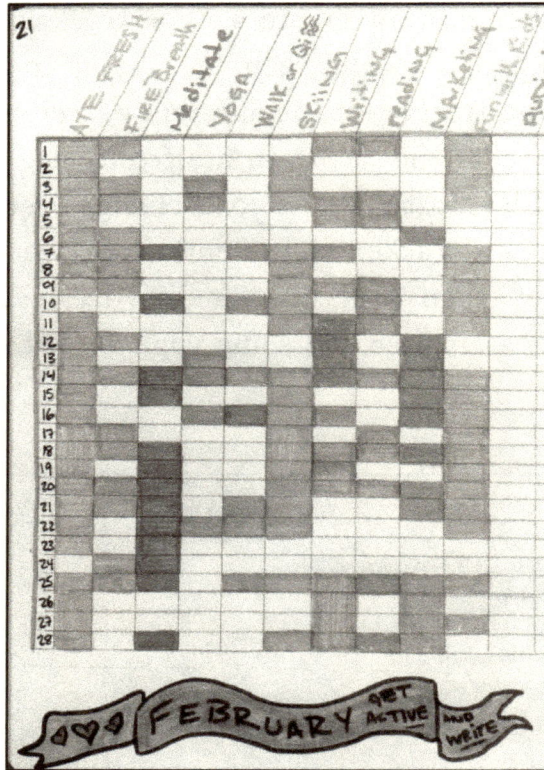

You can find tons more inspiration online. Just remember — your bujo is all about YOU, for you, by you. Don't be intimidated by someone else's picture-perfect journal. Have fun with it. Play around and find your own style. Sometimes I enjoy making my journal pages pretty, but I want things to be simple and easy to stick with, too, otherwise I would never be able to keep up with it.

Other things you can have in your bullet journal include shopping lists, plans for trips, story outlines, business ideas, income trackers, savings planners, reading lists, movies or series you've watched, miles you've run, songs you like, daily sketches, things your grateful for, and motivational quotes. I love making pages in my bujo that look like bookshelves lined with blank books. Each time I read a book or listen to an audio story in my car, I write the title down on one of the spines.

I think one of the most genius things to include in any journal is "The Year in Pixels," originally created by the Camille, a French blogger who goes by the name @passioncarnets on Instagram. At the start of each year, on one page in your journal, create a grid with twelve columns and thirty-one rows. Along one side name the months; along the other number the days.

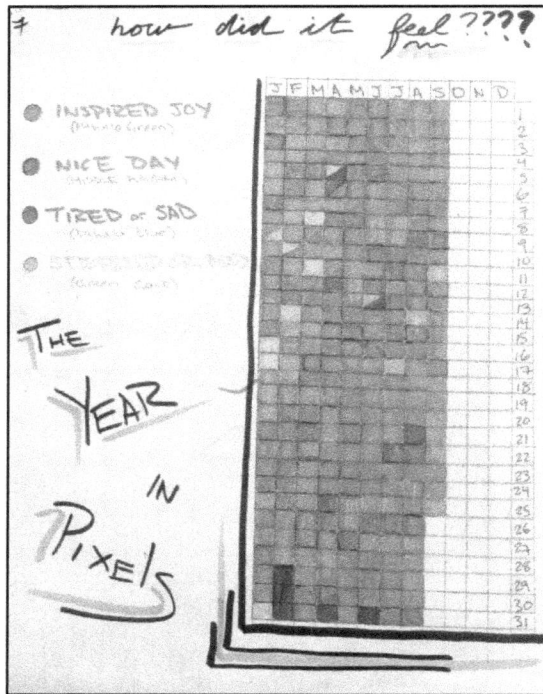

The Year in Pixels allows you to get a snapshot of your physical, emotional or mental state over the course of an entire year. Maybe it's just because I used to be addicted to Tetris®, but looking at this simple little tracker always makes me happy. It's a great way to identify patterns, see how things are working for you, and decide if you need to make any shifts in your routine. Each day you will mark down the dominant emotion or state for that day. Choose what states you want to track and assign each one a color. For sanity, I suggest keeping it to ten or less. Personally, I like to track four basics: Was I filled with a sense of inspired joy for much of the day? That's green. Was it a generic, nice day? That square gets colored pink. Was I sick or tired? Mustard Yellow. Angry, Stressed or Sad? A deep blue. When I look back over the year I can see how I've been feeling and what sort of habits I might need to change if I'm not happy or healthy (this year has been full of inspired joy!) Evolution is a constant, continual process. Over weeks, months and years, your passions might shift and your priorities will evolve. Your moods will change and every day you'll become a little bit more of who you were meant to be. The three practices outlined in this chapter can help you navigate those changes with less confusion and more focus so you can shine even brighter.

Seeing and Speaking Your Truth

Remember when I said that your soul is always trying to talk to you, but it's hard to hear over all the white noise in our brains? Freewriting isn't the only way to hear your inner voice. Your emotions can be a great indicator, too.

Most people think that when they are sad or angry it is because they are in a bad situation or something went wrong. But what if I told you that the reason we become sad or angry is more often because of our reaction to the situation and not the situation itself? When you judge a person or situation negatively, you create a natural disconnect from that person or thing. Negative judgments always stem from a place of dualistic thinking, so a negative judgment lifts you up and puts the other person down, polarizing the system. This is a flawed mindset, of course, because everyone and everything are part of Source so everything is part of the light and should not be judged in this way. Our emotions are a direct link to our soul, so when you are sad, it's because your soul is sad. Your soul is always connected to Spirit, so it does not want to polarize itself. It does not want you to judge an experience as lacking because it signed up for this experience, chose your body, chose your life. It's committed to the experience, and it would like you to be, too. When you're happy, that's a sign that your soul likes what you're thinking about. In many ways, your soul is like the "Yes Man" that Hollywood has made several movies about. It wants you to say yes to things, to remain open and expectant so that you can reach for joy again and again. If you are pushing back against your experience it becomes harder for your soul to guide you through life and even more difficult for the universe (Source) to figure out what experiences it should send you next. The more you dwell on the bad in your life, the more the universe thinks you are interested in that sort of experience...so it sends you more!

It's not always easy to shift out of grief and blame, but it can be done. I find the best thing to do with any experience, good or bad, is to throw myself into it fully. I start by expressing all my emotions — I cry, I hit my punching bag or pillow, I take a walk, I write down my frustrations and talk them out with friends, people I trust who know how to listen. Then, I make a plan of action, starting by figuring out what I would like to happen and outlining steps I can take to get there. Then, I focus on pivoting towards satisfaction. If I can get to joy, that's even better, but in a pinch I'll settle for just comfortable.

If we're not comfortable in our bodies, in our homes, it's very difficult to stay open to the abundance of the universe. Everything starts with ourselves. If you're not sure what to do or how to move into a better emotional space, try asking your soul. It's easy. Say you have two choices. You can spend the night reading or you can go to a movie with your friends. All you have to do is spend a moment thinking about each choice.

Imagine yourself reading. Take note of how your body feels. Did the idea spark joy or a feeling of expansion in the center of your chest? Did your shoulders hunch in a bit, compressing your breathing, or did you get butterflies in your stomach? Your body will give you physical cues in response to your subconscious emotions — feelings that are actually memos from your soul. Now think about going to the movies. How does that feel? Note again how the emotions elicit physical responses. A "yes" will always feel expansive while a "no" will make the body constrict. One choice is limiting, the other will lead you further down the path your soul is rooting for — the path with a heart, the path that will ultimately be the most fulfilling.

Of course, as a teen, you can't always choose what your home or school is like, but you can choose what you do while you are there. These days there is a lot of talk about how important it is to stand up for other people and not just stand around when we see or hear something that isn't right. The concept of being an upstander isn't new but it is gaining momentum. A long time ago, people lived secluded, simple lives. You hunted. You gathered. You worried about yourself first, family second, and everyone else never. Then, humans began to band together, forming nomadic tribes. The clan became an important convention of civilization. You protected your extended family, cousins, aunts. Then, humans started to form villages, cities, countries. Our circle of empathy grew, national pride took root, and we cared not just about our families but our communities, our people. Now, we have the internet and empathy has expanded in ways never before see. The world is actually a much safer place than ever before, but it still feels scary because we care about the people we connect with across the country and half a world away. Injustice is becoming less and less tolerable. We expect all humans to be treated with dignity and fairness, not just our own tribe, our own people. The time of the bystander is coming to an end.

That's where being an **upstander** comes in. An upstander is just what it sounds like — someone who stands up rather than standing by. When we see someone being treated badly, we always have several choices. We can stand by (watch the abuse unfold), go get someone who can help, step in and try to diffuse the situation, or confront the bully head-on. One of the easiest ways to help another person is to just stand next to them and start a conversation, ignoring the bully. It's non-confrontational and most bullies will back down because you've changed the script and they don't know what part to play next. This is so often the case that the US military now requires all their troops to attend upstander-workshops so that they can have training in diffusing situations within their own ranks. If you think stepping into a situation might result in physical harm, then the best thing to do might be to run and get a teacher or step away and call the police or trusted adult.

Sometimes being an upstander also means sticking by someone. If a friend is in a relationship with another person that makes you uncomfortable, that friend might not want to hear anything bad about their new friend or partner. They might get mad at you just for mentioning the fact that Ty seems jealous whenever Jet hangs out with anyone else. You've heard Ty yelling at Jet and been surprised that Jet seems to always cave into whatever Ty wants. You're right to feel uncomfortable because Jet is being manipulated and verbally abused. You've already told Jet how you feel, now you can choose: walk away from the friendship, which is what Ty is hoping for because isolated people are easier to control, or you can stay in touch with your friend and keep an eye on the situation. If you do the latter, you'll be able to step up and say something to an adult or get your friends together to help Jet when it's needed.

This kind of social responsibility can be applied every day, not just when you see someone being abused. Studies have shown that being isolated is actually more traumatizing than receiving negative attention. That means that the kid sitting alone at lunch every day and going home to an empty house where her parents work late every day is suffering just as much as the one you see being teased at school or yelled at every night at home. It's a different time of pain, quieter and less noticeable, but it's still a problem. Social isolation eats away at people's confidence and can lead to pretty serious depression and anger issues. So, the next time you see someone sitting by themselves, gift them with one of your radiant smiles. Say hi. Ask them what their reading. Let them know that there's a place at your table. If your friends don't like you socializing outside your peer group, ask yourself if those are really healthy friendships. Remember, good friends should want to lift you up, not tear you down.

Upstanding isn't just for social situations. If you don't like the way the environment is being treated, you can write letters to your government, attend peaceful protests, or join a volunteer group that works to improve things. If you're upset because you saw a dog that had been abused on Facebook, maybe you can't help that dog but you can visit your local shelter and help out by taking one on a walk every week. This kind of right-action ventures into the subject of spiritual tithing. You might have heard of tithing before in social studies or at church — it's basically a fancy word for paying ten percent of your income to your church to support the mission. Spiritual tithing is different. Instead of supporting a religious organization that may or may not use the money to help others, you can consciously direct your personal actions to support mass consciousness, the earth collective. You can take a portion of your energy and goodwill each month and using it to uplift another person or the community at large. This benefits them, but it also benefits you because your actions are creating the world you want to live in. Some people call this "being the change you want to see" or simply "giving back."

Each time you give back you create a ripple of energy that flows outwards from you through your family, your friends, your community, and the entire world. A small action can eventually create millions of synchronicities that make it easier for more and more people to also feel good and reach for positivity. The universe takes notice, too. It sees you working for the greater good and responds in kind, sending you more opportunities and rewards. All you have to do is practice saying yes, stay open, and watch for those synchronicities, those beneficial coincidences, yourself.

Not sure where to start? As a teen, you might find yourself in a situation where there's really not much action you can take. You don't have a car, your parents aren't around to help you, and you're just trying to survive another day at school. That's okay. There's a great little meditation you can do that can help shift your mindset, wherever you are, whatever you are going through. Tibetan monks have been using it for hundreds of years, praying daily for the upliftment of all beings on earth, including themselves.

The Loving Kindness Meditation, also known as Metta Bhavana, is a simple and effective way to relax your soul and allow situations around you to improve. Metta, in the Pali language, means unconditional love, or love with wisdom. It is both a self-help meditation and a manifestation technique, all rolled into one. It expresses love and gratitude and it facilitates healing both on a personal level and in communities.

Multiple clinical studies have shown that the Loving Kindness Meditation has profound emotional and physical benefits. Researchers have found that it:

- Increases positive emotions such as love, joy, amusement
- Decreases depression, anger, and other negative emotions
- Increases feelings of social connection and satisfaction with life

- Decreases chronic pain, migraines, and PTSD
- Activates empathy and increases gray matter volume in the brain
- Soothes the parasympathetic nervous system
- Decreases implicit bias and increases compassion and helpfulness
- Decreases self-criticism and increases self-appreciation and love

Not bad, right? Even one short session will have an impact, and results over time are more significant and long-lasting. The method is simple. Relax, and think of three or four things you wish to bring into your life.

Here is an example:

May I be joyful. May I be peaceful and comfortable. May I be fulfilled.

Now relax, close your eyes, and repeat the phrases out loud for a couple of minutes, directing the words at yourself. A self-empowering variation of this would be to use the words "I AM" instead of "May I be" for the first part.

Next, repeat the phrases, but think of someone you feel thankful towards and direct the intentions at them.

May you be joyful. May you be peaceful and comfortable. May you be fulfilled.

Third, we think of someone we feel neutral towards, someone we don't love or hate, like or dislike. For me, this is often someone I haven't had much interaction with, say a clerk at the bank or a server behind the deli counter. It might be hard to think of someone who you feel neutral about because we are all so prone to judgment, but eventually, you'll be able to think of someone. Direct the prayer towards them.

May you be joyful. May you be peaceful and comfortable. May you be fulfilled.

Next, think of someone you don't like, maybe someone who is bullying you or giving you a hard time, and direct the prayer towards them.

May you be joyful. May you be peaceful and comfortable. May you be fulfilled.

Finally, direct the prayer towards mass consciousness, toward all humanity and all beings on earth.

May all beings be joyful. May all beings be peaceful and comfortable. May all beings be fulfilled.

It's simple, it's effective, and it can be done with both children and adults. Try it for five to ten minutes a day and see how it works for you.

Focused Prayer

Part of the reason the Metta Bhavana prayer in the previous chapter works so well is that it makes use of positive affirmations.

One of the most significant and insidious stumbling blocks to feeling comfortable in the physical world is a lack of self-love. If we cannot fully accept and love ourselves, it is impossible to open fully to Source and follow our true path. We are afraid that we will not be accepted. We are afraid that we will not be loved. We are afraid that we will not be valued. We are all capable of empathy, but we do not exercise it all the time. And, we are hardest on ourselves. We are, as many have said before me, our own worst critics. But in order to really tap into mass consciousness and be fully receptive to the good synchronicities that Spirit is sending us, we must be willing to open ourselves up and be vulnerable to the possibility that someone else may also tap into us. We are best able to tap into Spirit when Spirit is able to tap into us.

There are many ways to strengthen our self-love: **positive affirmations** are one of the simplest. A dear friend of mine has tapped into her own power by holding a **pendulum** (a crystal or pendant at the end of a cord) as she states "I love myself" over and over. The longer she says it, the more vigorously the pendulum swings in a circle – sometimes it even flies out of her hand! She has found that this amplified "love energy" is capable of clearing energy throughout her house and that it helps calm her children down when they are upset. Pendulums can also be used to ask yourself simple yes or no questions. Hold your pendulum gently in one hand and dangle it over the center of your other palm. Like anything else, make sure you tune in to the right frequency first, programming your pendulum so only your higher self, angels, trusted guides or Source can come through by saying something like: "Only my spark-of-god-self may communicate with me today through this pendulum." Next, say "Show me yes" and note which way the pendulum swings. Then, say "Show me no" and see how it swings. Now, you can ask any yes or no questions you like, keeping the wording as specific and simple as possible. Make sure that you program your pendulum and check the yes/no directions every time you use it.

Another great technique to increase your feelings of self-love is to **give yourself a hug**. Cross your arms and place your hands on your shoulders or on your ribcage under your armpits. Holding this position for 20 seconds or longer has been shown to release endorphins and calm the nervous system – same as a hug from another person!

As you hug yourself, say positive affirmations such as:

I love myself.

I am worthy of love.

I receive love.

I am love.

I am peace.

I release my worries.

I embrace the day.

All is well.

Once mastered, this technique can be used often to reaffirm your self-love, even if you hold the position for only a moment. You can also soothe yourself in moments of stress by rubbing your upper arms or sides as you state your affirmations.

Want to take affirmations a step further? Think about the things you would like to manifest in your life (a functional car, a happy family, good grades) and affirm their arrival several times a day. Like most forms of prayer, affirmations work best when you talk about what you want *as if it has already happened.* It might sound counter-intuitive but when you talk to Source about the things you bummed about, all it hears is that you want more of those bad things. When you thank Spirit for your happiness, for bringing you what you desire, Spirit hears you saying you want more good things and looks for ways to deliver them to you. It's called the "Universal Law of Attraction," stating that whatever you focus on, you will attract more of. Why does the universe work this way? Well, in non-physical reality, aka the Source dimension, there is no such thing as time. Desires are fulfilled instantly — or have already been fulfilled — because past, present, and future are all happening all at the same time. It sounds crazy to us because we live in a world with a concrete timeline...or so we think. Sometimes, if we're in the right mindset, fully connected to Spirit, we can tap into that ability to work with the timeline, slowing things down or speeding things up. Manifesting our dreams in ways we never would have imagined possible. This is why many gurus say not to worry about how you will get there, but to just imagine that you are already there. Put yourself in that feeling of achievement, and say some positive affirmations, and see how things around you begin to change. How you begin to relax into life. How exactly can you do that? Let's look at our examples and see:

Your car breaks down all the time. You're too broke to do much about it, but boy would you like a functional car. Prayer seems like a long shot, but what have you got to lose? Imagine yourself driving down the road in a fully functional car and say the following affirmations:

I have a great car that always works.

I love my car. It takes me to the best places.

I am so grateful for the wonderful car I drive everywhere.

I appreciate how my car feels when I'm driving it.

Is your dad stressed out, is your foster brother driving you crazy, is your cousin depressed? Try these kinds of statements, even if they feel like a lie. Try to imagine yourself surrounded by a peaceful, supportive, loving family and *feel how that would feel*, then say:

I have the happiest family. We are all comfortable, healthy and happy.

I am grateful for my family. I love how everyone is kind and supportive when I get home.

I have the best times with my family.

Is school stressing you out? Are you having a hard time with some of your courses? Imagine yourself getting back papers with high grades on them and how great that would feel. Really see yourself in that moment and say something like:

Staying organized is so easy. I have no trouble handing in my assignments and getting good grades.

It feels great to do well in school.

I am so grateful for my teachers and the things I learn each week. My mind is expanding and it feels amazing.

I love making plans and hitting all of my goals. I'm excited about what comes next.

If you don't feel like positive affirmations are going to be enough to help shift the conflict in your home or community towards peace, the modern version of **Ho'oponopono** might be just what you're looking for. This traditional Hawaiian tribal healing technique was adapted and taught publicly throughout the 1980s by Kahuna Morrnah Nalamaku Simeona and made even more famous by Dr. Stanley Hew Len and Joe Vitale in the last decade. Kahuna means "light of sacred wisdom" in Hawaiian and was used to denote a healer, shaman or leader — anyone who was connected to Spirit and using that connection for the good of the community. Simeona was born in 1913, and her mother was one the last Kahuna Lapa'au Kahea, a revered healer one who used words to heal, and it was she who taught Simeona about ho'oponopono.

Traditionally, Ho'oponopono would occur in a relaxed family setting. If one person acted out or needed healing, the entire family or group affected would be considered in need of healing, and an elder would be called in to perform the ho'oponopono ceremony. The shaman or elder leading the exercise would walk the parties needing healing through the exercise in an informal round table discussion format where each family member could ask forgiveness from the others. As a group process, ho'oponopono has tremendous power. Simeona simplified the process to the private repetition of four short phrases in private, recognizing that modern western culture was suffering from fractured tribal and family communities and that healing was sorely needed on an immediate, personal level.

Simeona said, "We can appeal to Divinity who knows our personal blueprint, for healing all thoughts and memories that are holding us back at this time. It is a matter of going beyond traditional means of accessing knowledge about ourselves. We are the sum total of our experiences, which is to say that we are burdened by our pasts. When we experience stress or fear in our lives, if we would look carefully, we would find that the cause is actually a memory. It is the emotions which are tied to these memories which affect us now. The subconscious associates an action or person in the present with something that happened in the past. When this occurs, emotions are activated and stress is produced."

Modern ho'oponopono involves four steps. First, we acknowledge that what has transpired in our life has been allowed by the distortion of our own thoughts and memories, apologizing to ourselves for allowing those thoughts to pull us from our true path through poor speech, mind, and action. (I'm sorry.) Next, we ask Spirit and our own higher self to forgive us, releasing us the cycle of distortion. (Forgive me.) Then, we express gratitude for our life experience on Earth and for the opportunity to be healed. (Thank you.) Finally, we express our joy through our love for Spirit and ourselves. (I love you.)

Hew Len used the technique when he worked at the Hawaii State Hospital in a ward for mentally ill criminals. As he tells it, every day he would sit in his office looking at each patient's file and repeating the four ho'oponopono phrases. Within a few months, major positive changes had occurred and within a few, years the clinic went from being over-filled with difficult, violent patients to having the majority of its long-term patients rehabilitated and released.

The technique is easy but powerful. Simply repeat:

I'm sorry.

Forgive me.

Thank you.

I love you.

Try using ho'oponopono for a few weeks and see where it takes you. You might find it useful to write out the situation you are trying to improve or find a picture of the people you'd like to get along better with and place you hand over the picture or statement while you practice. Focus is an important part of conscious creation: your results often have less to do about the tools you use or things you do than about your intention.

In life, you always want to begin with clear intentions. Whatever you intend, you will achieve. If you want to do something, but do not believe in it with every fiber of your being, you will not have an easy time achieving it. The key is intent. Intent is more than just sort of, kind of, wanting to do something. Intent is about really wanting it. Really meaning it. Intent is about clarity of purpose, single-mindedness of will. As Yoda so aptly put it in Star Wars: "Do, or do not. There is no try." Never set out to "try" something. It most likely will not get finished, or progress will be harder than it should be, since the word "try" is related to the punitive words trial, or test. Set out to do everything, and things will get done. An easy way to work with developing your intentions is to simply state them by beginning any visualizations with the words "I intend to..."

Intention is everything.

Quantum mechanics has proven that all particles are essentially pure energy with no tangible matter. The closer science looks at matter, the more they find that there is nothing there. At an atomic level, we are empty space. When you look closely at an atom it is literally 99.9999999999999% empty space. The rest? It's a nucleon, which is also 99.999% space made up of quarks. These quarks, too, are 99.999% space, and so on, down to infinity.

We are space. We are energy. Each of our bodies contains enough energy on an atomic level to provide power to .1% of the entire world's population — that means 1000 bodies have the energy to power an entire world. 1000 bodies. What if we harnessed our souls, instead?

We are simply holograms, energetic constructs operating in a theatre of divine creation. Our energy flows through space as waves and particles, interacting with other waves and particles to create the response that we are expecting. To create our physical reality. Physics has demonstrated time and again that matter behaves as we expect it to. When we watch an experiment, whether "we" are human eyes and ears or simply a mechanical recording device, we alter the behavior of the particles that comprise our physical reality. If we want a photon to behave as a particle, it will. But if we want it to behave as a wave, it will do that, too. Which is it? Which are we? Physical being or spirit and energy?

The simple answer? We're both. It is the will of our soul, our intent to create, that decides what that means.

So, what will you create next? Positive affirmations are great, but if you're feeling crafty I have a couple more ideas for you. The first is what I call a **blessing box**.

The blessing box, also known as a prayer box, is an enchanted, empowered, awakened object that works for you 24/7. It's a place to store all your prayers, dreams and well-wishes while it hugs them and nestles them with love. It is an extension of you, a physical manifestation of your heart and your will that can help create the reality you are wanting.

A blessing box can be as simple or grand as you want. It can be a shoebox or a glitter-bedazzled creation. Some people, instead of using blessing boxes, have blessing books: journals where they inscribe the names of people whom they are praying for or goals they are working on. My own blessing box is painted and decorated with stones and feathers to help anchor each intention and give it wings. But that is me. Your blessing box should incorporate the things that make you smile and strengthen your intention.

Once you've created your blessing box, it's easy to use. Write down what you want on a piece of paper and drop it into the box. Remember to keep your statements positive and affirming so that you're working with the Law of Attraction, not against it. When you write your prayers, it's often best to leave them open-ended, so that miracles can manifest in their own way. If you want to, you can anoint the prayer with essential oil or perfume or write your wish with a particular color pen that feels good. Put aside a little time each day to simply hold the box, thinking about your prayers and expressing gratitude for their fulfillment. Remember, in Source's eyes, it's already happened. You are a conduit for the blessings. Know, expect and allow Spirit to create the best outcome, with highest good for all. Keep the box near your bed or on your desk, since just being near your blessing box helps power it up, and the more you see it, the more you are likely to use it. Fill it with prayers as needed, and every few weeks go through the box, removing the blessings as they occur.

The second tool I love to play with for manifesting the life I want is called a **vision board**. If you've ever had to make a poster presentation for school, you're already familiar with the basic technique, although vision boards are way more fun. First, you need to figure out what vision you are trying to create. More money? A happier life? A great car and apartment? New friends? Next, go through old magazines or search the internet for images that represent the vision you are trying to manifest. Collect all the pictures that you want to print, cut and paste. Get your glue and a piece of sturdy paper (I love to use pretty square scrapbooking pages or construction paper), and start pasting! Be creative and have fun. You can cut out or write inspiring words and messages on the board, too. When you're done, hang it up somewhere you can see it all the time, so you'll constantly be reminded to set that positive intention.

If you want to amp up your blessing box or vision boards even more, there is a special kind of toning you can do to energize and awaken them so that they will be even more powerful.

Transfigurational toning uses the combination of the voice, Source light and focused intent to empower, bless, cleanse or awaken an object or person. Call up your intention or vision, see yourself filling with the light of Source pouring through the top of your head and flowing through you, then allow both the light and your vision to blast out through your mouth with your voice, washing over the object with love, the power of Spirit and light. Your voice is all about creative potential and communication – it's what it exists made for. When you let the sound come and flow as it wants, miracles can happen. When the voice ends its song or tone, the work is done and your box or board will be empowered and blessed by Source.

Learn to focus your intention in a way that you simply believe and expect that which you are willing into being, and it will become that very thing.

Finding Your Quiet Place

The modern world is a loud, busy place. Sometimes your mind can go into overdrive, overstimulated by all the sights, sounds and ideas. Bad news on the television. Scary movies at night. Expectations at school, peer pressure, and that hungry velociraptor in your brain. Do you ever find yourself wishing there was a place you could go where you could just turn it all off?

There is. It's a little hard to find sometimes because you have to get past that velociraptor. Deep inside you, in the quiet darkness, you have what I like to call your inner still point. It's the center of your being here on earth, the center of your will to create, and it's an amazing place where you can become a god within your own body. Go there, and your velociraptor will get in line. Your thoughts will recede. And, with practice, you'll be able to get some really great guidance.

First, though, we need to get you there.

Your velociraptor guards the gate, but she's actually pretty easy to tame. Start with nice deep breaths in and out. When you breathe in, you take in good energy, powering up your body and repairing cells. When you exhale, imagine all the worries of the day leaving your body, all toxins you've accumulated dissolving into mist and light. Breathe in, and breathe out. If you like, you can use the four-fold breath — it's a perfect technique for calming the mind and body as it stabilizes your nervous system.

You might think you are terrible at meditating, but you're actually already doing it. Good job! People think when you meditate you can't have any thoughts at all, but that's not really true. There are many, many ways to meditate. Japanese Zen philosophy teaches us that the real struggle is not to shed our thoughts entirely, but to simply be in the moment. Single-mindedness is a great life skill, and being Zen can help you get there. Zen wants us to simplify things. When you are eating, just do that. Focus on the food, take your time, pay attention to the flavors and textures as you chew. If a thought train comes chugging into your head, don't jump on it, just think to yourself, "Huh, there's a thought." And let it go. When you are mowing the lawn, focus on the grass, the hum of the mower, the birds in the trees. Again, when a thought comes in, just label it, "thought" but don't follow its progression. And if you do, don't beat yourself up about it. Just return to your task. Get back in the moment. Part of the reason Zen practices encourage fewer belongings and clutter is because outside clutter encourages inner clutter. A very cluttered space often shows us that we've rushing around, hurrying through life rather than living in the moment and really paying attention to what we are doing. When every act is a conscious meditation, life takes on a natural order of its own.

Life IS the meditation.

You are the meditation. No really, you are! Read it again. You are the meditation.

We've talked about using positive affirmations before, but really, there is nothing more powerful than working with the phrase: **I AM.** Known as the lost word, the name of GOD, the name of all that is creation, the I AM gives you all the power. No one else can define your I AM. Only you. The I AM is everything that is you. It is your center, your truth, your power, your divinity. The words you attach to your I AM can free and empower you, or they can weaken and cage you. Choose carefully.

All day we attach words to our I AM without really thinking. We're not in the moment, we're not paying attention. As teens, especially, it can often feel like we're spending most of our time just trying to swim upstream where everyone wants you to be. Everybody says a lot of things we don't mean, especially when our inner velociraptors bare their teeth. But words have power. The I AM is power. Spending a few minutes consciously assigning words of power to your I AM can have a significant impact upon your day and your reality. It is the most powerful affirmation technique you can employ.

You are love. You are light. You are compassion and gratitude and thankfulness. You suffer because you judge yourself. You have removed your purity of heart from the equation, and each time you catch yourself doing something that you judge "unworthy" of the light, you distance your true self, from your own purity. There is no perfection. There is no light or dark. There is no right or wrong. There is only you, and you are perfection. Every moment you are in the perfection. Every moment you are the light. Every moment you are everything. Do not remove yourself from the equation. Your self IS the light. Release the struggle and the judgment and the search, and simply BE.

One of the best meditation practices you can begin involves affirming your I AM. Start each day with some good breathing, then quietly remind yourself of everything you are and want to be:

I AM love.

I AM purity.

I AM the light.

I AM the wonder.

I AM the perfection.

I AM the everything.

I AM happy

I AM healthy

I AM wealthy

I AM wise

I AM relaxed

I AM comfortable

I AM

I AM

I AM

You can add more positive statements here, but you get the general idea. You may also incorporate this meditation with the Metta Bhavana from the previous chapter, too, for a nice well-rounded practice.

Not convinced Zen mindfulness is for you? For years and years, I thought I couldn't meditate because my mind never, ever stopped. When I discovered guided meditations and shamanic journeying (more on that later) a whole new world opened up to me. It was like dreaming, except I was awake, and I could do whatever I wanted. Guided meditations are great if your thoughts are zooming all the time because they actually give you something interesting to think about. Instead of focusing on your breath or letting your thoughts float away, you are given an idea, a story, and asked to follow it. Want to give it a try? Here's a nice meditation to start with, one that's especially helpful for when you're feeling confused or tired. To listen along, grab your headphones and head to www.mayacointreau.com/transform/inspiration.mp3.

The Temple of Inspiration

To begin this journey, take three deep breaths.

Breathe in. Breathe out.

Breathe in. Breathe out.

Breathe in. Breathe out.

Feel your body relax. With each breath in, feel yourself go deeper and deeper into yourself.

Breathe in. And out.

Sink deeper and deeper, into the darkness.

All is still. Quiet. Dark.

Feel yourself becoming smaller and smaller, part of the darkness. You feel safe here, content.

Breathe in. And out.

In the darkness, stars glimmer all around you. They twinkle at you, happy. Joyful. You feel light and buoyant. Anything is possible.

You feel open and free. In the distant darkness, you hear a bird in flight. It is so dark, you hear it better than you can see it as it approaches. She flies nearer, and you see she is huge, large enough to carry you on her back. You climb on, and take off, into the night.

As you fly fast through the dark, you see something, a building, in the distance. The structure grows quickly as you approach, and you feel elated, excited.

The bird lands next to the building, which has the words glowing in the above it: "The Temple of Inspiration." The words dance and flow, free in the air.

Here you can be inspired. This is a temple of knowledge and wisdom, a place to come when words and ideas fail you. Here we can remember who it was we came here to be, to rekindle our enthusiasm for life and its many paths. The Temple of Inspiration feeds us possibilities and holds all that is needed to create and manifest our dreams.

Enter the Temple of Inspiration, explore freely, and open yourself up to new experiences.

Relax and enjoy. Take as much time here as you need.

When you are ready to return, leave the temple, fly through the night sky on the back of your bird, back into your world and into your body.

Mind Body ABCs

You are here on earth to experience the physical realm fully and gloriously. In order to fully understand the ideas in this book, we should discuss how energy and Spirit work in and through the body and introduce you to some terms that you might not be familiar with. Chakras. Meridians. Energy Centers. Wheels of light. Tree of life. Caduceus. Don't worry. It's not all that complicated. Just a quick little chapter and we'll have you spinning wheels of light with the best of them.

Your physical body is surrounded by the biofield, a larger energetic cocoon or aura that creates and holds the manifestation of your physical body. Just as your physical body has organs, arteries and veins, the energy of your biofield flows in distinguishable patterns. In India, they describe this with the Tree of Life and Chakras. In China and Japan, energy flow is discussed in terms of the meridians and energy currents (Qi or Chi). Everything works together to explain the way that energy flows through your body, keeping balance and maintaining optimum levels of health.

Let's start with some hard science first, things that have been proven through regular scientific method and observation. The body is energy and this energy is measurable at a distance from the body. Our energy reacts with and affects the world around us. Not only does our body emit heat and sound through its electrical and physical activity, but measurable levels of light! We are all walking around giving off approximately 100 watts of infrared radiation, as well as hundreds of thousands of photons of every second – low-level light.

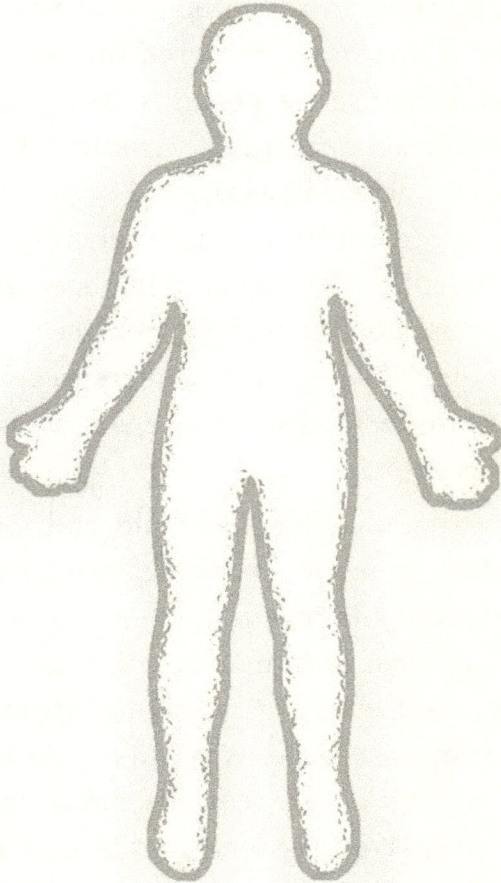

So can we really measure the aura? This intangible thing called a biofield? Well, scientists have been using SQUID magnetometers for over 35 years to quantify the biomagnetic fields of humans. Scientists at MIT and other universities have verified that not only does each organ in the body emit a distinct, measurable field of energy, but also that energy healers and Qigong practitioners emit the full spectrum of frequencies needed for cellular repair from their hands when they are participating in active hands-on healing. Scientists such as Reinhold Voll have measured the electrical status of meridians and acupuncture points and found that they do indeed have definite, measurable variations in frequency or flow. Furthermore, when an associated organ is debilitated or the person is in proximity to a harmful substance, readings will drop significantly. This research has been used to grow an entire field centered on the biofeedback one can receive from such instruments, allowing practitioners to easily determine whether a vitamin or food substance will actually benefit or harm a specific client.

Did you know that all adults and children have stem cells in their body called "somatic stem cells" which are capable of renewing dying cells and regenerating entire organs from just a few cells? Still, most of humanity continues to sicken on a regular basis and our organs don't always regenerate themselves perfectly. We die. Why? Many people believe it's because our energetic blueprint becomes corrupted, that death is a dis-ease. We take medicine to heal ourselves, but modern allopathic medicine is not designed to recalibrate our blueprint, to balance our energy or etheric shell. Our cells can not heal themselves because we are, on an atomic level, distorted. It sure would be nice to know how to re-balance that energy, wouldn't it?

Let's start.

The ancient Sanskrit word **chakra** means *a point of energy or power.* The earth has chakras, the body has chakras, the universe has chakras. In our bodies, energy flows not just to and from the heart in the form of blood, but through and between our cells on sub-atomic levels, within and all around us. The body has many small power points where this energy gathers, stabilizes and grows before moving on, from the crown of the head to the palms of the hands and the tips of the toes. The largest chakras are known both by their location and by numbers denoting their order of ascent on the body. The higher upwards you travel, the higher the number of the chakra. For our purposes here, we will be focusing on nine major chakras and their associations.

Chakras are often described as colorful, spinning "wheels of light." If your chakras are spinning well, they are "open" and you have a healthy energy flow. When a chakra slows down or stops spinning, it is described as "closed" or "blocked", which can lead to de-stabilization and dis-ease within the body. Qi in the body needs to flow clearly and regularly in a circuit. If part of the field is blocked, other places in the biofield will eventually suffer, much like the heart suffers when an artery is clogged. First, the chakras closest to the blockage will be affected, as well as the physical organs related to that chakra. Eventually, the entire system suffers.

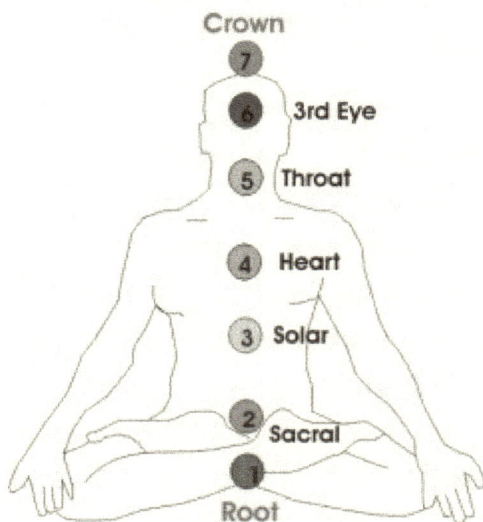

Our chakras help us gather, transform and utilize the energy around us. Source energy – the universal energy that flows through everything – and Sun Energy enter our bodies through our highest chakra, located at the top of our head. The chakras below that in our head and upper torso help step-down that energy so that our physical body can use it for cellular function lowering the pure Source energy into physical energy that our body can work with.

First Chakra (Root Chakra) At the base of your spine, deep within your pelvic area, the root chakra is the center of your intent to live. It governs your immortality and fuels your ability to ground and collect energy from the Earth. Your root chakra is what keeps you safe, what shields you from disease and physical harm. When it is damaged, your life-force is endangered. It is primal, sexual, survival energy. Think of the issues that Paleolithic humans would have been concerned with — the first issues. This is their chakra! It is associated with the colors red, black and brown, earthy tones. It affects the legs, bones, reproductive system, feet, and large intestine.

Second Chakra (Sacral Chakra) Here in your lower abdomen is your intent to feel with all the senses and levels of your being. This has to do with the connection you have to your family tribe or community and how secure or appreciated you feel. As Paleolithic humans began to band together in small tribes, our circle of empathy grew but so did our social anxiety and need to fit in. You might not want to be so sensitive, but more connected and sensitive you are, the more easily you may perceive imbalances in your non-physical self and repair the problem before it manifests in the physical. It is associated with the color orange and rules the lower back, genitals, hips and small intestine.

Third Chakra (Solar Chakra) In your solar plexus, your third chakra is the center of many people's energy and strength, involving your ability to protect yourself through the creation of positive boundaries. Issues of ego, fear, and instability tend to land here, as this chakra relates to your personal power and ambitions. Nomadic tribes, gathering into city-states and nations faced the same issues. In many ways, this is the chakra the world is seeking to balance as a whole right now. It is here that Joy and Solar energy is used to balance our incarnation, and so this chakra is associated with the color yellow.

Indigestion is a common symptom of unbalance in the third chakra.

Fourth Chakra (Heart Chakra) In the middle of your chest at heart level is your fourth chakra, housing your intent to love and accessing unconditional love. Unconditional love manifests in the world as a compassionate flow of energy from your heart chakra. As we move out of a world centered in the third chakra perceptions, we reach for a world governed by empathy and connection. When this happens, love and compassion bless all of creation with the love from Spirit, and we are open to receive unconditional love ourselves. This chakra is associated with both pink and green, pink for love and green for healing. Problems of the lungs and heart are symptoms of its imbalance.

In the past, the lower and upper chakras used to blend predominantly in the third chakra, and it was here that people would experience disconnection to their upper halves, but as humanity opens to unconditional love on mass levels, we are becoming centered in our heart chakras, and experiencing splits more and more in our throat chakra. These "splits" result from imbalances between our spirit, beliefs and ideals, and our physical, ego/earth-driven selves, and are best healed through the heart.

Fifth Chakra (Throat Chakra) Your fifth chakra is centered above your clavicle bone in your throat and houses your intent to create, harnessing the flow of Qi from Spirit and allowing you to manifest your dreams. If your will is not flowing, if you find you cannot speak or acknowledge your truth, your ability to dream and manifest is likewise impaired. The intent to create helps you bring your creative desires into physical being and is associated with clear, bright blue. Ley lines and energetic grids are most often seen as electric blue, too, when they are bringing in stable Source energy. Communication or informational related issues often manifest as sore throats or laryngitis, and can even affect the teeth and sinuses. When we have mastered fourth chakra reality we will enter into a new timeline where we can manifest our desires with ease, bridging space and time.

Sixth Chakra (Third-Eye Chakra) Your sixth chakra is your third eye. Unlike what you may have seen in pictures, it does not just reside above your eyebrows between your eyes. That brow point is merely the frontal portal to the third eye, which actually resides in the center of your brain in the pineal gland. The rear portal is at the zeal point at the base of your skull, and if you draw a straight line between the brow and zeal points, you will find the pineal halfway between it. The Pineal gland literally acts as a third eye, registering light and translating that into hormonal and chemical demands for the brain. It also houses your intent to see. When you intend to See you see the true reality of the universe, and the illusions of mass consciousness fade away. You will see your way clearly, and things will tend to fall into place. It is associated with the color violet or indigo and blockages here can manifest as headaches, eye strain, sleep disturbances, or ear infections.

Seventh Chakra (Crown Chakra) Your seventh chakra is located in the crown of your head towards the back where your soft spot was as an infant, and is where you have the intent to receive wisdom and evolve. It is where you receive Source energy and direction from your higher self and your biofield. When this center is impaired, it is more difficult to receive the correct information you need to maintain a high vibration and stay on the path of evolution. It is associated with the color white or gold, and is where you receive Ki or Chi from the universe. Crown chakra issues generally manifest as mental disturbances, confusing thoughts, and apathy.

Above and below the body you have two more chakras of note, commonly called the *Earth Star Chakra* and the *Soul Star Chakra*. Your Earth Star Chakra helps connect you into the Earth's living matrix, aligning your energy with the energy of Gaia and all beings for your highest good. Your Soul Star Chakra is the higher gateway to your higher mind, your soul and all of Spirit.

Meridians are Qi pathways in the body. They allow the energy in your biofield to flow from organ to organ, muscle to muscle, in a regulated, cohesive manner. Each meridian, like any line, is made up of an infinite number of points. Many of these points refer to specific organs or places in your body – just as each meridian regulates the flow of energy in specific areas of the system. When a point is blocked, the Qi becomes stagnant or blocked, and illness may present in the body. According to Traditional Chinese Medicine, gentle palpation or massage of specific points can often initiate movement and flow. Likewise, specific herbs and remedies are used to awaken the energy.

There are 20 primary meridians and close to 650 acupuncture points used in traditional meridian therapies such as acupressure and acupuncture. Reflexology is a very accessible derivative of this science and focuses on the points in the feet which have correspondences throughout the body. Try giving yourself a foot rub each night, paying special attention to any sore spots on each foot and see how your body relaxes and shifts over the course of a week.

In Ayurveda and the Kabbalah, the **Tree of Life** is more than just a creation story: it represents the human biofield. Universal energy is depicted spiraling down the staff of life, the caduceus, from the top in mirror waves, winding back and forth like two snakes in an image that reminds many people of DNA.

At the top, or head, we have Source energy as it enters the body. The staff itself represents the energetic core of the body, the spinal cord, and the Central Nervous System. It is the neutral core or pole of the body, and holds the blueprint for physical form. Where the energy begins in the head and aura, the poles are reversed, with the masculine on the left side and the feminine on the right. As it crosses down into the body, the right side of the body is generally considered masculine, while the left side is feminine. The right is positive, yang, stimulating, expansive, restless and conscious. Paternal issues tend to manifest on the right side of the body. The left side is negative, receiving, contractive, dreamy and yin. Maternal issues manifest here.

As the energy expands and flows downward in both its feminine and masculine, or negative and positive aspects, it crosses several times, forming fields of energy as it travels down through the body. Each of these fields is related to a different element, a different energy, and corresponds to a different element governing part of the creation of physical life. Where the fields meet problems can most easily arise, causing congestion and stagnation.

All of the aforementioned energy systems seek to describe one thing. Our biofield is alive. It is a complicated web of energy. No one part of our body is truly independent of another. Every cell works together with a group. The better our biofield is functioning, the healthier and happier we will feel. And the better we feel, the better life can be.

Keeping everything in top shape is as easy as saying your **ABCs**.

Activate...

Align...

Balance...

Clear...

Connect...

Stabilize.

Quiet your mind and center yourself with some deep breathing. Lift one hand and place the palm over your brow; place your other hand over your abdomen at your belly button. Paying attention to any sensations in your pelvis, start with your first chakra and say:

I activate, align, balance, clear, connect, and stabilize my first chakra.

It may take two seconds or twenty, but you should feel a slight shift in that energy center, a positive aligning. Then, focus on your lower abdomen and repeat:

I activate, align, balance, clear, connect, and stabilize my second chakra.

Again, wait until you feel that "click" of energy settling into place. Then, work your way through all your chakras. End by saying your ABCs for your earth star chakra, your soul star chakra, and your aura, too. Once you get the hang of it, you'll see it's a very quick method that can be used just about any time you are feeling out of sorts, over-stimulated or vulnerable.

Say your ABCs every day and watch yourself grow more relaxed and confident as the weeks pass. Your body will feel more comfortable, and so will you!

Heaven and Earth

Have you ever watched a martial arts movie and marveled at how hard it is to knock the hero off his feet? Martial artists spend years master horse stance, standing with their legs wide and bent at the knees, strengthening their connection to the earth. The practice helps them build power in their legs and balance in their core. It makes them strong. In horse stance, a fighter is better able to handle whatever comes their way and defend themselves without retreating.

Wouldn't it be nice to be able to do the same every day, wherever you are? You can, and I'm going to give you some grounding techniques to get you started. Grounding is a term borrowed from electrical engineering. In your house, electrical wires are grounded so that the electricity won't run all over the place, setting fires and shorting out circuitry. If there is a power surge, say from a lightning strike, a proper ground ensures that your home won't burn down. In the body, grounding helps us regulate and optimize the flow of Qi coming in from Source and connect to the physical realm of Earth. Grounding keeps us balanced, comfortable and empowered. Sounds good, doesn't it?

Let's get started.

One of the simplest ways to get grounded is with a **walking cleanse**. You can use this method anytime you are walking or exercising, whether you are indoors or outdoors. You could even do it in PE when the teacher has you running laps! As you walk or run, pay attention to your breathing. Imagine that the air you breathe in is pure, perfect, clean. As it enters your aura, any pollutants are purified by the white light that surrounds you. Every breath fills your body with energy, oxygenates your lungs and emboldens your soul. You are pure light, and every breath you take makes you lighter and lighter, pulling in more and more energy from Spirit through the top of your head at the crown chakra. Every time your foot hits the ground, imagine excess energy pulsing off of you, releasing in small atomic bursts. Grounding the bright flow of Qi entering your body through the top of your head and flowing through every cell. As you raise your foot up back for the next step, you draw the energy of the earth to you, into you. Connecting with the gridwork of the earth, of mass consciousness and threading your own higher self deeply into the web of life. You are grounded. Clear. Free.

If you can walk around outside barefooted, even better! Barefoot walking, or **earthing**, allows us to benefit from earth energy at a cellular level. Scientists say walking allows us to discharge positive ions into the earth, something our body was naturally designed to do — too bad we wear shoes, dampening this great function. When we walk barefoot we also draw **negative ions** into the body, increasing serotonin levels in the brain and helping us stay healthy. If you'd rather not walk barefoot, you can also soak up lots of negative ions at the ocean, near waterfalls, or on top of a mountain — all places where water molecules get smashed apart and release negative ions by the thousands.

Stuck indoors for a while? Try **imagining you are a tree**. Any type of tree will do. Take a moment to imagine yourself swaying with the breeze, standing tall and strong. Sit straight and tall, and breathe deeply. Imagine you are taking in air through all your pores, not just your lungs.

Feel the oxygen entering your bloodstream and clearing out debris while it energizes your entire body, cell by cell. When you breathe out, toxins and stale air leave your body.

Breathe in and out.

Now imagine you have roots flowing out through your feet, your root chakra, your spine. Visualize a long taproot reaching far down, down into the earth. Feel the earth alive and pulsing with energy all around your root, the energy flowing freely up the root and into you through the soles of your feet and your root chakra. The earth energy flows up through your chakras, through your body, and connects you to the Earth. You feel loved and connected. As the earth energy flows through your body, through your torso, your head, your arms and legs, it relaxes you and releases feelings of stress and anxiety you've been storing on a cellular, muscular level. Any stressed or tired energy you have flows is released down through your root chakra, through your taproot, and eliminated into the earth. You sense the cells of the earth, the organisms living in the soil, are eager to be nourished by this energy, and that they will use it to create new, clean energy for you. Allow this circle of energy to flow for several minutes, taking in the clear energy of the earth, and releasing your old, tired, used energy to feed her and be renewed.

When you feel completely clear and recharged, thank the earth, gather up your taproot, and return. This is something you can do in class, watching TV, or in your room. Even better — go outside and sit on the ground with your back against a strong, healthy tree. Trees love working with humans, and the extra energy can give you a real boost!

You can ground while you eat, too. There are lots of **foods that help ground us**. Although all foods are, on some level, grounding, certain foods are better than others at stimulating the root chakra, while other foods work better for the higher chakras. Also, keep in mind that each body is different. Your body may react differently to certain foods than the rest of your friends or family. Always attention to what works for you.

Generally, root vegetables and high-protein foods are the most grounding. Potatoes, beets, carrots, turnips, celeriac, eggs, meat, nuts, and beans are just a few examples of such foods. These foods help seat us firmly in our lower chakras and fuel us with large amounts of grounding earth energy. Dried foods are also very grounding, whether they are meat, vegetable or fruit, due to their archetypal connection to survival in the mass consciousness. To clear your root and sacral chakras, eat spices like horseradish and hot peppers, garlic and onions. On the sweet side, sugar and honey are also grounding and calming, while chocolate literally repels negative energy. Salty foods, and salt itself, encourage our ability to receive energy from the earth and the sun, and let our body's energy centers flow as intended. Dairy will slow the flow of energy within the body, helping those who have an over-abundance of energy running through them to better utilize the information they are receiving. Dairy can also reduce energy leakage and enhance psychic reception.

Using certain colors and materials in your **clothes or decor** can also help you ground. Try wearing earth tones and natural fabrics derived from plants or animals to help you connect to the earth. Your furniture, the color of your walls, all of these can have a profound effect on both your biofield and your mindset. A room decorated in forest-like colors can be as nurturing as the real thing, helping you rest and recharge, especially in the dead of winter or the high heat of summer.

Stones, used properly, are an obvious and powerful choice both for grounding and protection. Of the earth, they are good channels for free-floating energy. The key is to pick the right stone for your purpose. A meteorite may be beautiful and intriguing, but it is not going to bring you back down to earth. Pyramid-shaped stones, like naturally-occurring apophyllite or carved tetrahedrons, raise energy and open the crown chakra to the heavens, but do little to connect that heavenly energy to the body's lower extremities and down through the earth.

I recommend that everyone who works with stones always have a few good grounding pieces on hand. The stones listed here are some of my favorites for providing consistent earth energy. They are both steady and clarifying. They might not be the most exciting or sparkling gems in the case, but they will remain faithfully yours: virile, protective and strong allies.

All **agate** is gently grounding, and soothes and calms the nerves. It helps build confidence and self-reliance. Agate comes in almost every color, each of which corresponds to different chakras to further help with chakra specific issues.

Black tourmaline allows you to get to the root of problems and negativity. Black tourmaline in particular is a grounding stone with very high vibrations, and shields the wearer from negativity of all kinds, including electromagnetic waves and radiation.

Possibly my favorite grounding stone, **bloodstone** activates the root and heart chakras and draws energy from the earth directly through the legs and reproductive organs, dispersing energy equally throughout the entire body via the circulatory system and the meridians. It is a comforting, protective stone that brings calm and reassurance to the wearer, lowering the heart rate and blood pressure while soothing the soul.

Calcite is a gentle, friendly stone that helps clear disturbances in energy fields be they geopathic, electromagnetic, or in the body. Use calcite to clear your energy when you feel you are picking up too much energy from people around you, or when you are over-stimulated.

Calcite comes in many colors and opacities, but the clear or translucent varieties are best for this purpose.

Carnelian energizes the physical body and stimulates healthful activity while grounding. Excess energy from the upper chakras is transmuted by carnelian into physical strength and vitality. This beautiful reddish to brown stone helps facilitate a constant exchange of this energy with the earth, allowing the wearer to become one with her surroundings. Negativity rolls off the back when one bears this stone, making the bearer impervious to ill will from others. It helps heal wounds of the heart and body.

When our souls are still not sure that incarnating was the best idea, **danburite** helps us feel more comfortable in our bodies and brings us back to reality while facilitating an open channel to our higher selves. The pink pieces have a particularly soothing effect, though all danburite is calming.

Deep, dark red **garnet** is very similar to bloodstone in its properties, with its healing effect more focused on the blood and sexual organs rather than the entire body. It has the further effect of enhancing sexuality and virility, and is one of the best stones to awaken and open the root chakra.

Hematite is a very yang, or male, stone of a dark silver color. It works very well with men to protect them from negativity and balance their testosterone. Reflective yet magnetic, hematite will draw negativity and illness off of the bearer and reflect it back to whence it came. For this reason, it needs regular weekly or even daily cleansing depending on the intensity of its use. To cleanse Hematite, place it in a bowl of cold water in a window overnight.

Kyanite clears and aligns the chakras of all those who come near it. When it is worn, it has a constant protective and grounding effect as it clears and aligns, clears and aligns, over and over again. The bearer of this stone is quite difficult to knock off-balance energetically. Because the chakras are aligned and open, one's higher self and energy body are able to better interact with the physical body, leading to higher ascension and attunements.

Obsidian is one of the most grounding, protective stones you can find. Obsidian looks opaque but is actually translucent, which helps allow us to see through the negativity to the positive, and vice versa, to see what is hidden. Apache Tears are a particular variety of obsidian that is steeped in legend, and has the added quality of helping one cope with issues of anger, grief, and forgiveness.

Labradorite brings all chakras and layers of the body into alignment while strengthening the aura. It refines DNA and allows your soul to feel more comfortable within the confines of its physical body and this dimensional reality. When the physical and spiritual aspects of yourself are in harmony it is easier to remain calm and peaceful, secure in your own true self, you can meet the day with assurance and ease.

Onyx can be found in many earthy colors, including brown, green, and black. Long used as a popular stone for men's jewelry, onyx has a warm, safe, feeling. The green can be mossy or brilliant, and is good for healing and connecting to nature. Brown onyx helps energy flow up and through the root chakra, and remediates many reproductive issues. Black onyx is good or shielding one from negativity and lending the wearer courage and strength.

Petrified wood is not a stone, per se, but ancient wood which has fossilized over the millennia to form a light, stone-like substance. Jet is a form of black, petrified wood that has been used in jewelry for centuries. All petrified wood helps root us to the earth while filtering out toxic thoughts and patterns from our DNA, much as live plants filter and purify the air and water, which passes through them.

Passed through the aura and around the body, **selenite** will cut cords and remove energy drains. Placed in a room it will clear geopathic and electromagnetic stress, as well as any other form of negativity. It is so good at clearing that the stone itself never needs to be cleansed, as it will never hold negative energy itself.

Tiger's Eye is a beautiful, striped stone of golds, browns, blacks, and blues. Sometimes it takes the appearance of a hawk's eye, in which case it is believed to increase insight and understanding in the owner, while the golden examples are used in homes and businesses to increase prosperity and abundance. All tiger's eye is very protective against psychic attacks and ill will, and helps protect travelers. Few are foolish enough to mess with a tiger, and the big cat energy that is held in this stone will hold vigil over those who carry or wear it.

Are You Grounded?
Take the Test

The following test is not definitive, but it is helpful in determining if you are grounded. Answer these questions and then we'll score your answers.

Do you find it hard to pay attention when other people are talking?

Do you feel ruled by your emotions?

Do you get distracted easily?

Do you need to chew gum to help focus?

Do you find you often multi-task (ie: watch two videos at once)?

Do people say you are spacey or have ADD?

Do you think about the past more than the present?

Do you stumble often or have many accidental injuries?

Do you find it difficult to wake up in the morning?

Are you prone to road-rage or other disproportionate anger?

Do you stress out easily?

Do you sleep more than 12 hours a day or less than 7 hours?

Do you avoid decisions or wait for signs to make all your decisions?

Do you feel uncomfortable in your body?

Do you over- or under-eat?

Do you have a hard time following instructions or directions?

Do you forget what people said to you?

Do you find yourself places and wonder how you got there?

Do you have a hard time being on time?

Do you watch more than 2 hours of TV at a time daily?

Do you have a hard time distinguishing your dreams from reality?

Scoring the Test

Each "Yes" answer denotes an element of un-grounded thought patterns or behavior. Everybody is a little ungrounded from time to time, it's only natural when so much of our being is rooted in both spirit and on the earthly plane.

If you gave more than a few "yes" answers, you should probably do some simple grounding routines on a daily basis. Something that can really help here is to **tighten your silver cord**. The silver cord is like an umbilical cord connecting our soul to this physical incarnation, a representation of our intent to remain here on earth in our body. When you feel at sea, imagine that you have a fishing rod and are reeling your cord back in, making the line nice and taut as it stretches from your energetic body up to Spirit, to your higher self – most see the cord emanating from your umbilicus but you might also see it elsewhere, such as your zeal point at the base of your skull or the crown chakra on the top of your head.

Positive Protection

Have you ever found yourself stepping away from someone who has gotten a little too close during conversation? Do hugs make you uncomfortable? Everybody has their own parameters for **personal space**, the buffer zone we like to keep around our body. It's an ancient phenomenon, one that science has been studying for decades. All animals have a concept of personal space; it's part of our hard-wired defense system that keeps us aware of predators. Personal space is like a second skin that helps us constantly monitor our surroundings and use tools more effectively. When you touch someone without their permission, brush against another person's body on the sidewalk, or stand too close in line, you run the risk of triggering their defense system. This can induce stress in the body or initiate a PTSD response, reminding them of a time when they might have been hurt or touched in a way they did not like. In general, you want to give people at least a foot of room when you're standing or sitting next to them, or a couple feet if you're talking face to face. Friends and family might feel more comfortable getting close, and some people will always want more space, so try to pay attention. If someone steps away, don't try to step closer.

Personal space requirements can change from day to day, too, contracting when a person is tired or stressed. If you need more space, you might need to do some work with your heart chakra or do some grounding work.

The heart chakra has a lot to do with personal space because it regulates how open we are to giving and receiving love. When I say love, I'm not strictly talking about romance. I mean unconditional love — the blessings, appreciation, and gratitude we can give and receive. When we have been hurt or feel vulnerable, or heart chakra creates a larger buffer zone for the body, impacting our physical preference for personal space and weakening our ability to connect with other people. We can work on this by strengthening and maintaining **positive boundaries**.

I know what you're thinking. Boundaries are walls. How can building walls help us connect in healthier ways? Positive boundaries are different. Positive boundaries have foundations of joy and lift us higher, while walls are built with bricks of fear, anger, and instability that crumble and make us tremble inside when they are breached. When we push someone away because we are afraid of being hurt, we're enforcing a negative boundary, a boundary based on negative beliefs and emotions.

You can start building positive boundaries by determining what sort of things you are comfortable with and saying yes to more of those. The clearer you are about who you are and what you want, the easier it becomes to interact with the world. Once we know what makes us comfortable, it is easier to identify what is not serving our highest good. Then, it's up to us to say no and mean it.

Saying no can be one of the hardest things for any adult, let alone a teen. From childhood, we are taught to behave and obey. Sometimes we might even have been punished for saying no or pressured to explain our choice. Caregivers and teachers are often guilty of this, but so are our friends. You've heard of peer pressure, right? That happens when the group does not uphold the right of the individual to say no, when the individual is pressured to do what everybody else is doing, even if it feels bad. Many of us have been taught that it is good to give up some of our comfort to make another person feel better, or to help a group maintain equilibrium. Often, we feel like we can't say no, even though we may really want to. We'll make all kinds of excuses and rationalizations to try and make ourselves more comfortable with saying no, all the while forgetting one very important thing:

"No" is a complete sentence.

Say it with me.

No.

No.

NO!

It's kind of fun, right? You don't ever need to explain yourself. The word "no" says it all. You don't need to say, "No, I don't want to do that" or "I'm really sorry, but I can't do that because my mom said I'm on probation." Remember, "No!" is a complete sentence. Practice saying no. Mean it. Don't let people think if they bug you enough you'll change your mind. If you're not really sure you want to say no, that's different. Say "I'll have to think about it" or "Maybe, I'll let you know tomorrow." Saying no and meaning it is an important part of maintaining your positive boundaries.

Respecting other people's right to say no is also important. You're here on earth with a planet full of other people and living beings, many of whom will be happy to join you along your path. Why waste time bugging one person to ignore their own positive boundaries? It's disrespectful, and you wouldn't like it if somebody did it to you. You want people to respect your right to say no, right? Make sure you respect their right to say no, too. We're all here to co-create — to manifest our dreams and visions through interaction with other people. If our souls wanted us to only work on ourselves by ourselves, we would have incarnated onto a planet all by ourselves with no other beings to play with. But that's not why we're here, so we need to get along and respect others, not force our will (or our bodies) upon anyone else.

Above all else, you must learn to **trust your own instincts**. For as long as there have been humans with different dreams, there have also been those who would abuse the act of co-creation. It is my very strong and personal belief that all abuses of power are detrimental not only to those whom the person would seek to harm, but also to the abuser. Forcing our will upon another person or taking away their power might make us feel good for a moment, but that power, those choices, belong to someone else and in the end, the abuse will have a detrimental effect on our own well-being.

What we send out always comes back to us.

It might return in the form of a life lesson, a loss of Qi energy that manifests physical dis-ease, bad dreams, depression, or even hope. It is my own hope that through our time together, you will learn the beauty and harmony of being in balance, how to energize yourself directly from Source, and how to realign yourself as needed, so that you can always walk the path with a heart, in line with your individual true soul purpose. It is my intention that the training you do with me will bring you to higher levels of confidence and self-trust, so that you can dance through life as the empowered light-being you really are, thus raising the vibration of all you meet, so that they can each do the same, and so on, and so on.

If you find yourself being easily swayed by your peers or feeling nervous and vulnerable, there are some simple things you can do to bolster your aura and strengthen your field of protection.

One of the most basic yet effective methods of protection is to imagine yourself surrounded by white light. Many traditions take advantage of the effect of a circle or sphere. To both protect yourself and raise your energy, I find a pyramid is most effective. Try the following exercise both ways and see what works best for you.

Visualize a white **pyramid or sphere of light** in front of you, and then see yourself walking into it. See the light seal around you. Set the intention that no other being can enter into this pyramid or bubble without your consent or that is harmful to you. You can also use this visualization to protect your house or the room you are in. To protect very large spaces, I find domes of light to be very effective. Sometimes you might see the light as another color, such as blue or purple. That is okay, too: my daughter makes her bubbles pink with rainbow sparkles! The key to creating an effective thought-form is your intent.

If you need help clarifying what your positive boundaries and goals should look like, go a little deeper with the following meditation with the pyramid of light: www.mayacointreau.com/transform/protection.mp3.

The Pyramid of Protection

To begin this meditation, take a deep breath, in through your nose and mouth.

Breathe out.

Breathe in, and breathe out.

When you breathe in, feel your lungs expanding, filling up with air. Feel yourself getting lighter and lighter with each breath, the air carrying you higher and higher.

Breathe in, and breathe out.

With each breath, your consciousness grows up, and out. Feel it expand.

See the air entering your body swirling with shades of purple, lavender, and indigo. See the purple tones of light enter your lungs and flow through your body.

With each breath, see the purple and lavender hues within you grow brighter and brighter. The light begins to flow through your crown chakra, your third eye, and your physical eyes. Feel yourself surrounded by beautiful indigo and lavender tones of light.

Feel yourself protected, surrounded by love. Out of the light, four brilliant white pillars begin to form, one in each direction. They rise high over you. Slowly, they move to form a pyramid structure over you. It glows with a beautiful, pure white light. These pillars form a haven of protection, which nothing evil can ever cross. You are very safe here. Nothing can harm you. Any time you feel in need of guidance, or protection, whether physical or spiritual, see the white pyramid of light in your mind, and enter.

Now, you are here in the center of the Pyramid of Protection. We have come here today to work on Intuition. We all have the power to intuit, the power to feel and divine. It is our birthright, a power we were born with. The power of intuition goes hand in hand with the power to create. It is what guides our hand as we dance through life.

Many of us have closed off our channels of intuition because we were afraid to see too clearly, afraid of being too open, too vulnerable. We may have been taught that it is dangerous to use our intuition, that it can lead us falsely. This has been a teaching of fear, and through it we have lost much of our power to create life as we dream. For without intuition, there is no guidance and without guidance, we cannot follow our own true path. We become like a ship without a rudder.

Here, in the Pyramid of Protection, you are completely safe. You are grounded. You are a clear channel. Nothing impure can enter here. As you sit surrounded by white light, see your breath flow lavender, indigo, and purple again. Feel your chakras open, your third eye open.

Breathe in, and Out.

Allow your inner mind to open, let your thoughts flow freely. Do not filter them, just let your thoughts come, and go.

Imagine yourself being guided by your higher self throughout your day. See yourself using your intuition, opening up your psychic channels, so that your days go smoothly, guided by a higher power, for a higher purpose. Your higher self, your true soul, wants only the best for you, and acts only out of love and compassion for you and for all beings. When you allow your intuition to flow freely, miracles may occur daily. Allow yourself to open to all possibilities.

Breathe in, and Out.

Imagine how a perfect day would go, and try to envision where you would like it to take you. See this happening every day.

Now see if your higher self has any messages for you, if you gain any insight into your current path, and where you are meant to be. Open your mind to every possibility. There is nothing you cannot do. You are pure, you are divine, and you were born on this world with the power to create.

Breathe in, and Out.

Remember that you can return to the Pyramid of protection at any time, just by visualizing a pyramid of white light, walking into it, and seeing the light seal around you, protecting you.

Thank your higher self, and ask it to help you as you learn to use your intuition. Ask it to teach you how to discern intuitive messages from those coming from the ego. Now see the pyramid around you opening, and you walk out, back into this room, back into your body.

You are whole. You are protected. You are one with your higher self.

When you are ready, return.

Have you done everything here and still feel like you need stronger boundaries? For really solid, earthy protection, try **grounding through a mountain**. Start off by imagining you are a tree, just like before, but visualize yourself on top of a mountain you feel connected to. Imagine your roots going down among the deep, substantial rocks that make the heart of the mountain. This can be a longer, more difficult process as your roots may meet with more resistance, but they will also connect you to the tough, immovable, extremely stable energy of the mountain.

Remember, intention is everything. You determine who or what is allowed to siphon off your aura (nothing should!). You determine who and what can connect with you and impact your energy.

If you're having trouble at home or school, don't forget to **talk to someone you trust.** School counselors, caregivers, and parents are supposed to have our best interests at heart, but if they aren't a good fit for you, maybe an aunt or grandparent can help, your favorite teacher, one of your friends and their parent, or a neighbor. There are hotlines, too, staffed with people who are trained to help, as well as social workers and law enforcement agents who might seem scary but usually have everyone's best interests at heart. Talking to a person we trust is a great way to co-create because they can help us lift our vibration and find solutions. Never, ever, feel like you are helpless or alone. Do not yield to fear or sadness, because that very feeling is a signal from your soul that you are not looking at things the right way. There is always a way out, we just need to look for the light and find it. You always have options.

"Fear has two meanings: Forget everything and run, or face everything and rise. The choice is yours." ~Zig Ziglar

Empath Problems

Today was bad. Your nerves caught fire, your head was pounding, and you felt like yelling at everybody. Maybe those bad feelings have something to do with that velociraptor in the brain but maybe...they're not even yours.

Don't get me wrong. I'm not a big fan of the blame game, and I definitely think it's important for everyone to take personal responsibility for their feelings and moods. Still, we can't escape the fact that when our biofield is connecting with the biofields of everyone else, our auras mingling as we sit in the same room, we often pick up on what's going on with other people. This is called empathy. Empathy is an amazing tool we all have that has helped us build bigger, stronger, better tribes and communities. Without empathy and compassion, we would be a lot less likely to help others when they need it because we wouldn't be able to imagine ourselves in their place. Some people don't just have a little bit of empathy, they are wide open to other people's feelings all the time. This is called being an **empath**. Empaths don't just feel what's going on with other people, they take on some of the pain themselves to help lighten the load. This might help other people, but it definitely doesn't feel good for most empaths. A lot of healers are proud to say they are empaths and take on other people's pains...until they get sick, too. Then, it's not so much fun. Could there be another way?

In a word, yes. It is time for us all to reach past simple empathy and towards true **compassion**. Compassion is a lot like empathy. In both situations, you empathize with the other person, but utilizing a compassionate viewpoint you don't actually dive down into the pain or despair. You can help your friends without getting sucked into the drama; you send money to save the elephants without getting torn up about the danger they are in, you smile and say hi to the new kid who seems really isolated, but you don't take his loneliness on as your own. You try to help, but you are able to remember that the pain is not yours even while you work to remedy it. The grounding and protection techniques in the previous chapters will help you a lot and allow you to filter out more of the drama.

Check in with yourself whenever you're feeling low and ask yourself: Is it mine? Is it someone else's? Is it everyone else's? Sometimes we pick up on something called **mass consciousness**, the group mind that extends like a web over the entire planet. There have been plenty of studies about group mind, and even though science isn't quite sure how it works, we do know that it does exist. Mass consciousness is a collective, the sum total of all the emotions and frequencies of all beings on the planet. If a lot of people are cleansing karmic grief or working hard to take the planet to the next level, it can feel like a drain to anyone who is sensitive to the energies of the earth. Again, shielding yourself on a daily basis and maintaining those positive boundaries can help a lot with this!

Sometimes, of course, you're just not going to feel good. You are a spiritual being in a physical body that is tied to the earth, and when the earth is having issues, you're going to feel it. There are times when the earth's atmosphere is more vulnerable to galactic and solar radiation, and we get slammed. Earthquakes, volcanic activity, forest fires, weather systems, tidal pull, and pollution can all have profound impacts on our bodies and psyches. **Geopathic stress** is real, and can be compounded by things like electrical magnetic frequencies, wireless signals, and cell phone towers.

Even though the pain you might be feeling isn't always yours, the work still starts with you. Anything that might lift your vibration will help — stay grounded and keep your vibration, your Qi, high by saying your ABCs and getting your own heart into a more positive space. Don't get sucked into dramas. When I'm getting bombarded by negative news or emotional input, I turn off the social media and disconnect. I get out in nature. I read a good book. I make myself a cup of hot cocoa and snuggle with my dog. Anything that makes you feel more comfortable is going to help. If you need to, let yourself have a good cry, go for a run or give your pillow a pounding. It's good to let out our negative emotions — it's not good to wallow in them. Like any rain-filled clouds, let them release their burdens and pass through. Then, turn your attention to more positive things and try to nurture yourself so that you feel more at ease. Never underestimate the power of a single personal act. Everything you do can help raise the vibration of your community, of mass consciousness and the earth. Each small act of balance shifts the web of humanity and helps to create a better world.

When our heart is strong, so are we. It's easier to handle the woes of the world and create a better world when we're more in balance. As an empath, this starts with the heart. It starts with your capacity to love and that always begins with self-love. One of my favorite places to learn this is the Temple of the Open Heart. It's a beautiful castle where you can visit countless rooms for healings, or just soar through the skies on the back of a giant eagle. Read through the meditation below and have a visit, or listen to the meditation online here: www.mayacointreau.com/transform/openheart.mp3.

The Temple of the Open Heart

To begin this meditation, you take three deep breaths.

Breathe in. Breathe out.

Breathe in. Breathe out.

Breathe in. Breathe out.

With each breath go deeper within your body, until you reach your inner point of stillness.

Breathe in. Breathe out.

Breathe in. Breathe out.

Deep within yourself find the quiet darkness where creation begins. Here, anything is possible. You are a god within your own body.

In the darkness, you rise up and begin to walk south. You find yourself in a quiet, young-growth forest. Aspens, birches, and oaks stand in every direction, and there is very little undergrowth. The trees are well-spaced, and you pass easily through the forest.

The ground is soft with leaves and moss, and your footfalls make little to no noise. The woods are cool, shaded by the leafy canopies high above you. Sunlight dapples the ground, and you catch glimpses here and there of a clear, blue sky. Every so often, you hear an eagle's cry high above the trees, muffled by the leaves.

You head down a gentle slope towards a sunny clearing in the distance, and as you enter the clearing you realize that it is far larger than you had imagined.

Before you, a wide meadow valley stretches far into the south, meeting gentle hills over a mile away. The skies are clear and the sun is bright, reflecting strongly off a large castle-like temple in the center of the valley. 10 tall cone-shaped towers rise 100 feet into the sky, with colorful banners streaming from their points in the wind. The temple is immense and made with white and gray stone polished to a high gloss. Three large blue doorways the color of the sky lead into the temple, and even from this great distance you can see that the doors stand open.

You have found the Temple of the Open Heart, and begin to walk across the meadow towards it. When you are halfway there, you find yourself walking a flagstone path that winds towards the temple.

On your left and right you can see other paths leading from the hills down to the temple, and you realize that there are paths stretching in all directions, radiating outwards from the temple to greet travelers and always meet them halfway.

You approach the main door of the temple. From the left door, a giant white eagle, taller than you, exits and takes off in flight. You enter the temple, and find yourself in a large, empty hall, with two great staircases leading up to a second floor and many doors leading off towards the side towers.

You stand in the middle of the hall and are approached by a tall, blond woman. Towering behind her, one of the temple guards and guides stands quietly, another white eagle.

The woman takes your hand and welcomes you. She tells you: "I am the keeper of the Temple of the Open Heart. There is much to see and feel here, and we welcome you. If you so choose, you may climb on the back of this eagle guardian, and he will take you to the sky and show you great mysteries, for all in this world is touched by and part of the Temple of the Open Heart. Or, you may stay with me, or walk through the Temple on your own. Each of our Towers holds a truth of the heart, and you can visit them anytime you want. Our doors are always open, for there are no boundaries to the Open Heart."

Explore, be healed, and enjoy. When it is time to return, return to the temple, through the forest, and back into your world and body, knowing you can always return, always find peace and upliftment in the Temple of the Open Heart.

Your Turtle Temple

Keeping your body balanced and clear is one of the best ways to stay grounded and energized every day. It's hard to stay happy when we're feeling sick, and hard to make healthy choices when we're unhappy. Everything we've talked about so far in this book will help you feel more balanced, but the body needs love and support, too! Your soul is like a turtle in its shell — one can't live without the other, and cracks in the shell, in your body, will hamper your efforts at a happy life. Disease is really about dis-ease, or our soul's lack of comfort in the physical world. An easy way to support your body is to look at what you're eating. Diet shouldn't be about the latest health fad or looking a certain way — it should be about feeling your best.

Your body is developing still, building bones, teeth and tissues, so **eating well** is especially important. What you eat now can determine how healthy your body will be later in life. Try to eat foods that are as natural as possible: whole grains, pesticide-free fruits and vegetables, natural sugars instead of chemical sweeteners and corn syrups. If you can't pronounce or identify the ingredients on a box, they're probably not that good for you. Cooking from scratch is always going to be healthier than anything you can get in a box, and you don't need to be a wizard in the kitchen. If the adults in your house don't trust you to cook on the range, see if they'll let you use a toaster oven! Stay away from the microwave if you can, because they've been shown degrade the nutrients and flavors of your food.

No matter how healthy your diet is, though, you'll always be taking in some toxins these days. Pesticides, plastics, antibiotics, and herbicides are in our soil, our waterways and the air, contaminating even the most pristine places. Does this mean you should just give up? Of course not. The more you can lower your toxic load, the better off you'll be and the more easily your body will be able to clear out the toxins it does encounter. This means your cells will be able to rebuild themselves properly day in and day out, your neurotransmitters will be able to fire at will, and, most importantly, you will be more comfortable in your skin. At Harvard, Herbert Benson documented Himalayan monks raising the temperatures of their fingers and toes by up to 17 degrees through meditation; monks in India lowered their metabolisms by 64 percent. If you can shift your metabolism, you can also shift how your body deals with toxins.

When you find yourself confronted with less than healthy food or beverage choices, consider employing your own willpower to define your experience. You define your reality. You assign the identity to the objects around you. Your frequency or vibration determines your life experience, including the aspects of matter around you. This is how fire-walking works, so people don't get burned.

Our expectations affect how matter behaves at a quantum level, our thoughts and words carry real power.

Atoms ripping through space and time create what we hear, see, smell and touch. They have frequencies that can affect the structure of water, literally imprinting it with their energetic signature, but they also react to the observer — matching their behavior to line up with our expectations. This is called "The Observer Effect" in physics, where the simple observation of a phenomenon will always change that phenomenon. Humans, machines, it doesn't matter: even instruments that measure experiments have been proven to alter the state of what they measure in some manner. So, how do we apply this to our environment and our dinner plate? Masaru Emoto carried out many experiments on water and the observer effect. His results showed the world both gorgeous and disturbing images of how our very thoughts can change the structure of water. The words "ugly" and "hate" create deformed ice crystals without structure, while words like "joy", "love" and "gratitude" transformed the same damaged water so that it formed crystals with the most intricate, breathtakingly beautiful crystalline symmetry — even an image of the Buddha himself! Taping words or placing objects in water has been found to alter its energy signature, which in turn can have a beneficial impact upon the cellular structure of the body. Praying over polluted water, likewise, has been shown to eliminate toxins. This likely is where the ancient practice of blessing waters and using them to heal the body first came into being. The things most people don't realize is that you don't need a priest or temple to consecrate your water — you are Source, remember? You are an instrument of power, glory and grace, even if it doesn't always feel like it. You can raise the vibration of your food and water, bless the animals and the plants, too. Use words of love and expectation to bless your food, put a peace sign sticker on your water bottle, or just put your hand over your plate for a moment (or under it under the table) and focus on clearing and stabilizing the energy there the same way you would balance one of your chakras. Speaking of chakras, you can also do some meditation work to alter your biofield to become a more effective toxic screen around your physical and energetic body, so that nothing can reach you without being cleansed of its own toxicity.

Don't forget to be happy when you eat, too. Our emotional state can affect how we process food and store weight more than any calories. My parents divorced when I was young and my father moved far away. Whenever I visited him, we would eat very, very well. Six-course dinners at five-star restaurants. Cheese platters and desserts at lunch and dinner. Pastries and hot chocolate for breakfast. I didn't have friends at his house to play with, so I'd spend a lot of my time reading. You would have thought I'd come home heavy and out of shape, but it was always the opposite. I'd almost always come home looking radiant and feeling great. I was happy when I ate all those tasty foods, relaxed and comfortable. If I get stressed now and stop eating or overeat? It doesn't matter how much I'm eating — if

I'm sad or afraid, I gain weight! When you are emotionally or mentally uncomfortable, your body will try to protect itself by padding its aura, and this is often reflected in our physical bodies.

Don't skimp on sleep either. You need to sleep every day, more so when you are a teenager. While your body is in standby, your brain goes to work, building and repairing. Your liver detoxifies your blood. Your bones grow. Your muscles heal. A lot of us sleep less during the week and try to play catch up on the weekends, but that doesn't really work for the body. Most adults need 7-8 hours of sleep every night to function at optimal levels; teens need 9 hours and fifteen minutes, according to most studies. Try not to spend more energy when you are awake than you are replenishing during the night. Don't confuse energy with excitement, so that when your excitement levels are high you do not sleep at all. When you do not sleep enough you are damaging your energy. If you want to be a powerhouse, you need a power source. You are like a rechargeable battery: your body also needs time to re-charge and download the energy it has received from food to enter into the other aspects of your self. Sleep. Eat. Do these things deliberately, and with intention. Do them as if they matter, because they do matter. They allow you to BE matter. And they allow you to materialize, to manifest and live a more fulfilling life. Creation takes energy, and to deliberately create, you must deliberately feed, house, and recharge your creative vehicle: your body.

There are **steps you can take to live better at home,** too. Try to choose furniture and clothing that is more environmentally friendly, looking for local options or recycling (buying used is great!) when possible. Cut down on the clutter in your room. If your room is really messy, so is your energy. Respect yourself and keep it clean. This will lower your stress levels by giving your brain less to compute, as well as give mold, microbes, and dust mites fewer places to spawn so that you can breathe easier. Then, ask one of the grownups in your house to help set up an **essential oil** diffuser and run it a few hours every day. Some plug into the way and heat up essential oils, vaporizing them into the air, while others use water to create an aerosolized mist to deliver benefits. Both work well. You can use any essential oil you want, just make sure it's pure essential oil, not cut with perfumes or thicker carrier oils like soy or sunflower oil which can clog up your diffuser.

All essential oils act as a plant's immune and defense system, so they are all antimicrobial, antifungal, and anti-inflammatory on some level. Lavender, patchouli, sandalwood, ylang-ylang and frankincense are calming and soothing, perfect for the end of the day. Peppermint, eucalyptus, thyme, rosemary, and basil are all great for colds and flus, and they will wake you up, making them great for study time or gaming. Citrus oils like bergamot, lime, lemon, and orange are happy, cleansing and uplifting. You only need a few drops in your diffuser at a time, so one bottle can last you a very long time.

Once your own space is clear and comfortable, think about taking some of that clarity out into the world, too. Some people litter, leaving the earth worse than it was before, while some work to **make the world better**. Which type of person do you want to be? There are lots of ways you can improve things in your community, small changes can have big impacts. When you see a piece of trash on the ground, pick it up. Consider spending an hour or two each season "greening up" community parks or the street you live on. Grab some friends or your family, a couple trash bags, put on some gloves and get some fresh air while you pick up litter along the road just make sure you wear bright colors and stay out of the street). You might even start picking up cans and bottles and taking them to a recycling center to make some extra cash each week. Not comfortable picking up trash? That's okay. There are lots of ways you can help the environment — sprout some trees from apple seeds or pinecones and plant them; talk to the adult who handles the bills in your house about signing up with their electric company to get some of your electricity from renewable providers; turn down the AC when you're leaving the house or set the heat lower when you go to sleep.

There are ways we can **contribute to a better social environment**, too. Always afford other peoples' bodies the same respect you would afford your own. The rules in life for interacting with other people are the same as they were in kindergarten: no hitting, keep your hands to yourself, and always ask first. Make sure when you touch someone, you're respecting their personal space and getting consent for things like kisses and hugs. You don't like it when other people make you do things, so don't force anyone to do something they don't want to do, either. Ask permission. Get consent. And don't do anything you don't want to do just to make someone else like you. If the person you like is pressuring you to have sex or make out and you're not ready, don't do it. Anyone who really cares about you will always respect your feelings. No one is going to love you more or treat you better just because you gave them what they wanted. All you'll really be doing is showing that you don't respect your own wishes — so why should they? When a person cares about you, when a relationship is truly balanced, they will support you while they support themselves, not demand that you value your own needs less than their own.

Your body is the only thing in this life that truly belongs to you. Treat it with respect and it will work hard to support you. Flood it with toxic food, drugs, and alcohol and it will get sick. Abuse it physically or allow other people to use it like a toy and your Qi will fade. Every culture on earth has references to the body as a holy thing, a temple. It's something to be cherished and valued, above all other things. So when you eat or drink, do it from a place of joy. When you make out with someone, do it because you want to, because you are ready and excited, not to fill a hole in your heart or to make them stick around.

Still not sure about what you really want or how to keep your body happy? You can **use your body as a pendulum** to check in with your soul and your body to see what choices they are hoping you'll make. Some people call this **biofeedback** or **sway testing**.

It's very simple. To begin with, you want to take a few deep breaths and balance your chakras, making sure that your energy is aligned. Stand up and bring your hands up to your heart center and rub them together briskly for a few moments while concentrating on connecting with your body and your higher self. The movement of the hands helps get your Qi flowing and aligns the left and right sides of your body. Now, drop your non-dominant hand to your side and bring your other hand (the one you write and do most things with) over your forehead, keeping it an inch or two away from touching your skin. Think of a yes or no question you'd like to ask your body, being careful of the wording. Next, slowly bring your hand down along your face towards your chest, still not touching the body. If your body sways forward, that's a yes. If it sways backwards, that's a no. Not moving is not a maybe! If the body doesn't sway as all, refine your question or try rubbing your hands together again, then ask again. It does not matter how much you sway forward or backward — the strength of your swaying is indicative more of your connection to the body and your higher self than the strength of the body's preference. A yes is a yes, and a no is no. Simple, right?

The hardest part, like with most things, is **asking the right questions**. Asking "Should I eat tomatoes with dinner tonight?" is not going to yield as high quality an answer as asking "Will eating tomatoes with dinner tonight contribute to my highest good?" or "Will eating tomatoes with dinner tonight make me healthier physically, mentally, and emotionally?"

Don't be afraid to break your questions down into different parts. Say you've been invited to go camping with a new group of friends, but you're a little nervous. You could ask questions like "Will camping next week feel good physically?" "Are there things I can bring or do that will make me more comfortable on the trip?" and "Is going on this trip going to benefit me emotionally?"

Sway testing can help us get to know our own bodies and souls better, and when we're better informed we can make better choices and enjoy life more. Better choices, better lives!

Colors for Your Soul

Sometimes the easiest way to see what is going on with yourself is to allow the body itself to show you. Not tell you – but map it out for you. On the next few pages, you'll find **body mapping** you can practice using. If you enjoy the process, make a copy of the provided body maps or draw your own.

To start, get out a rainbow array of coloring implements (crayons or colored pencils work great, just make sure you have a full spectrum of at least eight to twelve colors). Color in the dots on the body, as well as the body itself and the empty space around the body. Don't think about it too much, simply grab colors without conscious thought and color away. What you will end up with is an image that will show you what sort of issues are going on and affecting different parts of the body and the chakras, as well as a picture of the aura itself.

Use what you have learned about the chakras and the elements and their corresponding colors to intuitively decode what you see. By coloring both the front and back views of the body, you can receive a clearer idea of what is going on. Even if you can't quite "read" the drawings, you will have just given the body an outlet for expression, and that in itself is priceless.

As you're looking over your body maps, remember that there are no "bad" colors, not even black or gray. It is all just information. If you see blue in the root chakra, it does not mean that the chakra is off, but more likely that you are having communication issues about sex or survival – you might be looking for answers about these issues, talking about them a lot, or maybe you are helping someone else understand the topics better. Green in the third eye could mean that you use your intuition in sports or choosing what to eat, or that they make decisions based on their emotions rather than logic. Black can show grounding or protection, or something you feel strongly negative about. Gray may indicate sadness, but can also be about peace or confusion.

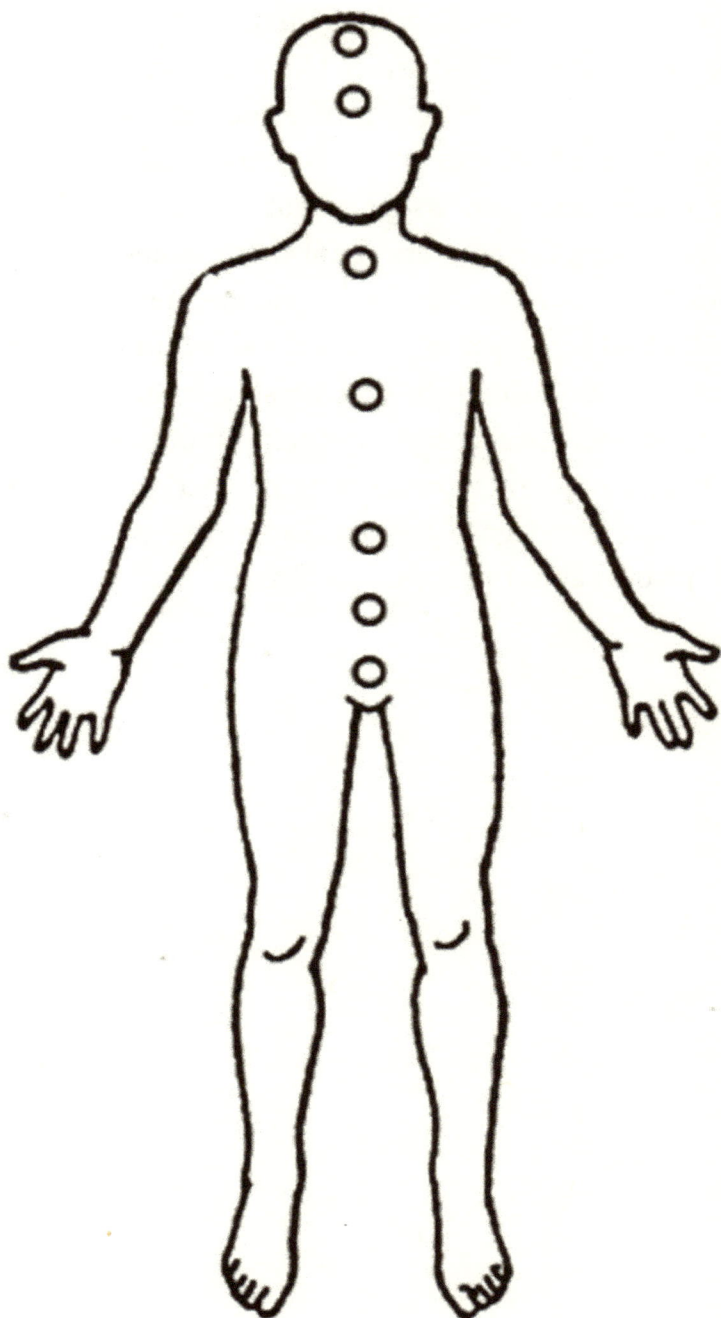

Maya Cointreau

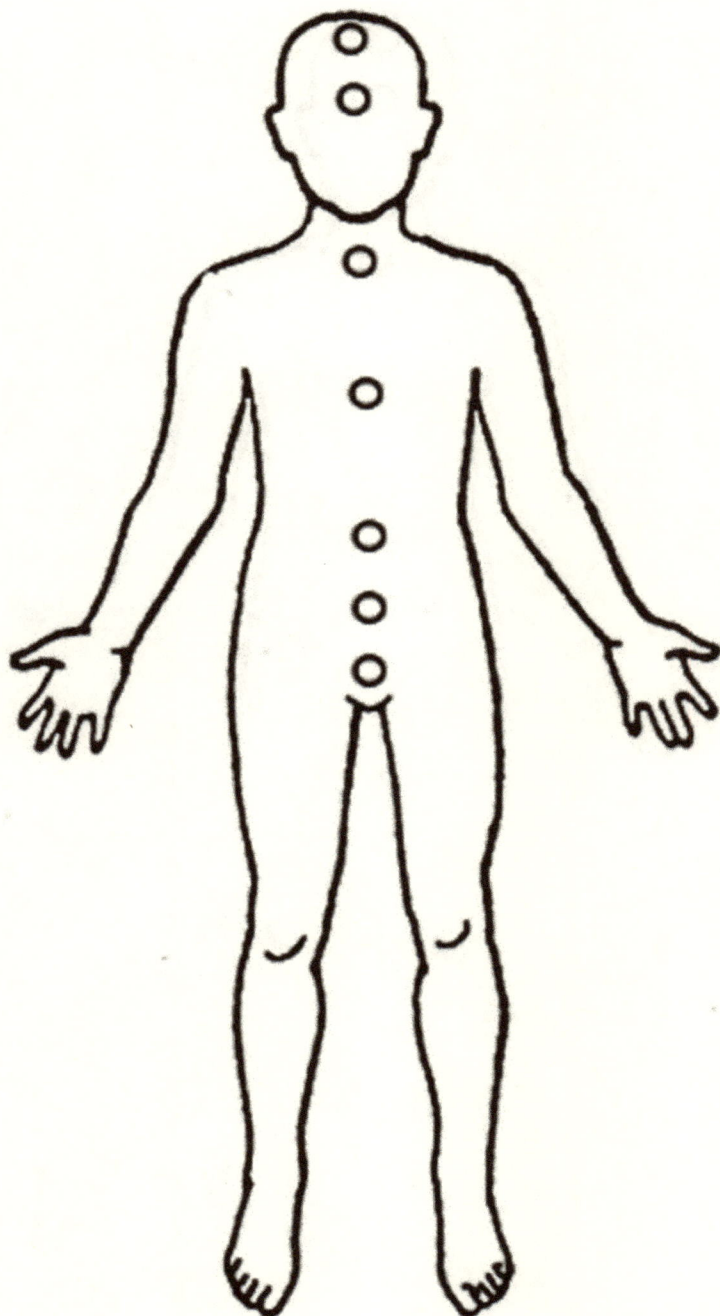

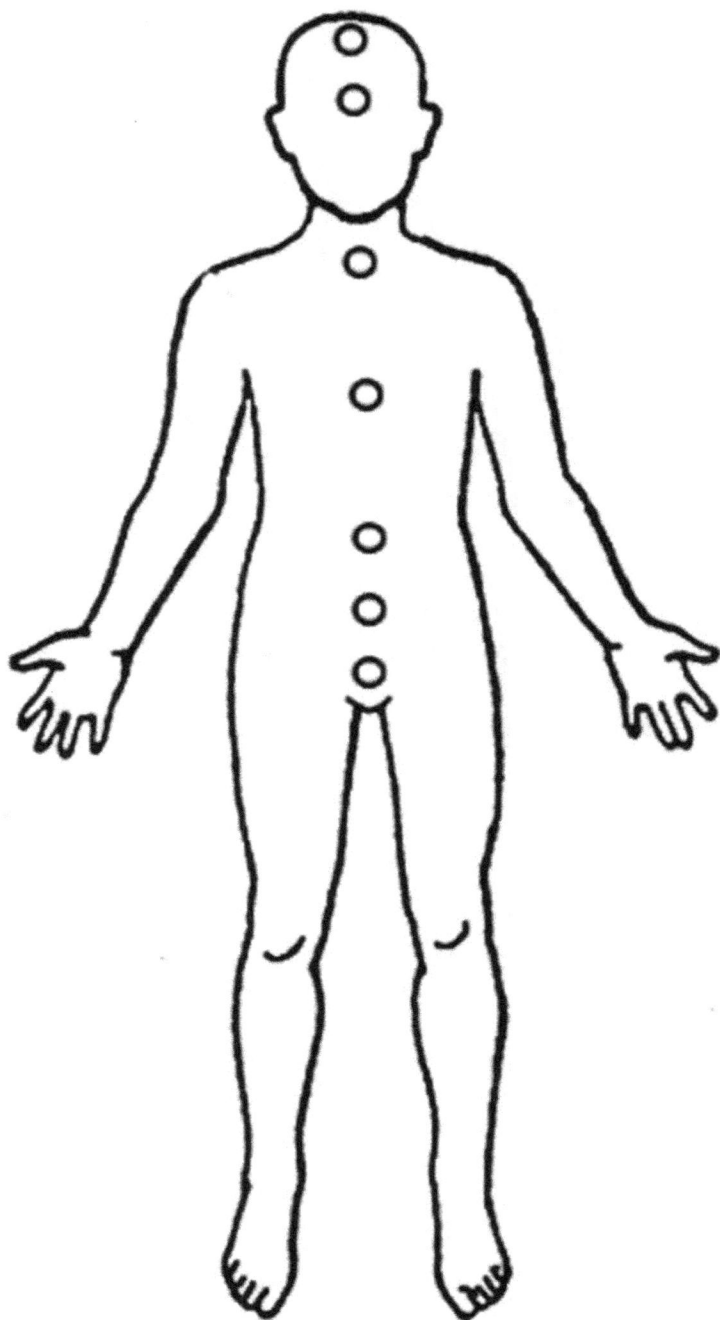

Maya Cointreau

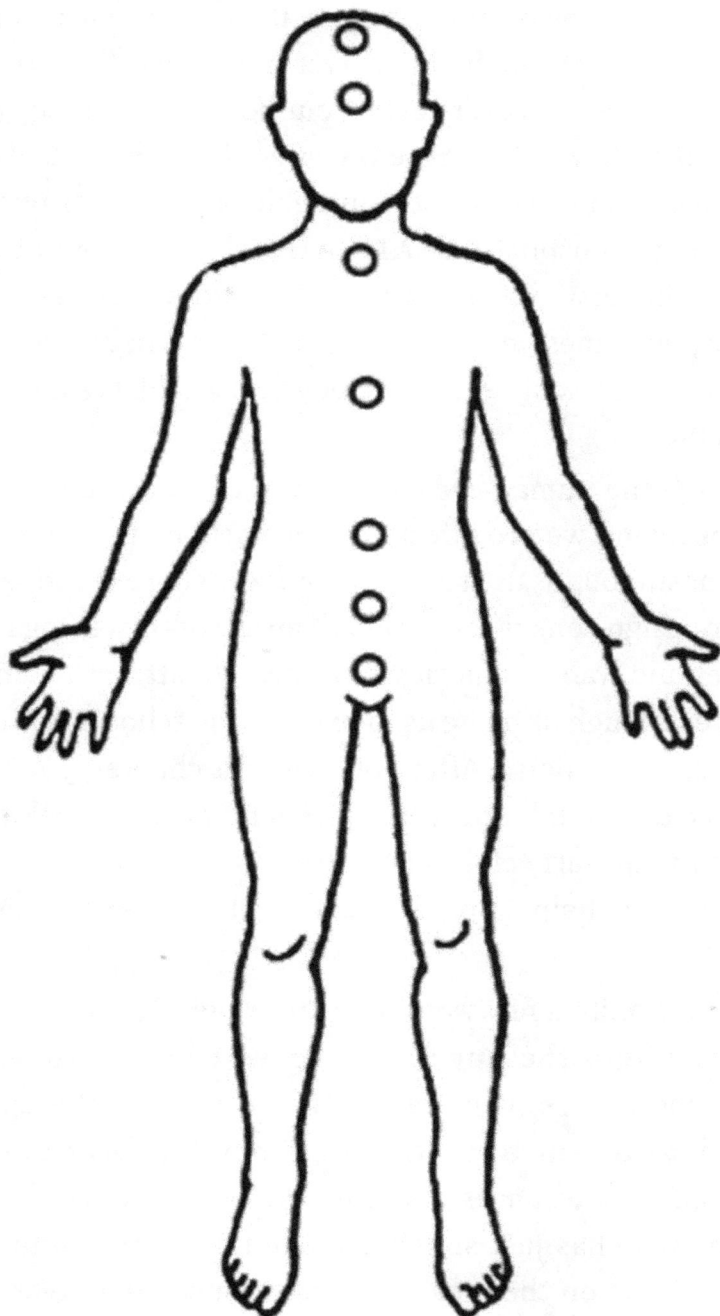

Color has its own superpowers: it is light, pure photon energy flowing through the universe in wave-like streams, and it resonates with every cell in our body. Multiple scientific studies have shown that these waves go through our body and are actually transformed into a useable form of energy called adenosine triphosphate, or ATP. ATP, in turn, is used by our bodies to instigate cellular repair, to process DNA and RNA, proteins, enzymes: everything our bodies need to repair themselves and exist here in the physical world. Light is, quite simply, life!

Although the human eye can see but a small fraction of the light spectrum, we are affected immensely by the colors and light that surrounds us at all times. Advertising executives and interior design consultants are well aware of this, using colors on paper and walls, in fabrics and wares, to attract us, engage us, make us laugh or bring us to tears. Some schools get it, too, but a lot of them don't. After you read this chapter, you might even decide to talk to your teachers or principal about organizing an art club to help harness colors in your classrooms to help improve focus and help everyone feel happier.

There are quite a few ways to harness light for healing, too. NASA uses **light therapy** to heal bones, benefit muscles and tissues, and relieve pain. Various forms of color therapy are believed to aid in a multitude of physical dis-eases and emotional disturbances. Personally, when I work with someone who has just suffered a painful injury, I often will place my hand on the area and imagine a cooling green light infusing it, soothing it. It's something I began doing instinctively when my first child was a toddler, prone to testing his body's abilities and getting new bumps and scrapes almost every day. I sensed most of his small bruises and injuries emitting a red glow, and found that visualizing the hot area cooling to green (the opposite color on the spectrum) would quickly help diminish my son's pain and even prevent bruises from forming. I've tried this with many people since then, adults and children, and still find it works very well. Blue light, on the other hand, seems to be better suited to chronic energetic disturbances and long-term physical issues. Every color can be appropriate and helpful in the right time and place. The key is to find what works for you.

Chromotherapy is the scientific term used for all applications of healing achieved through the application of color. Colors have been used as instruments of healing for over 4000 years, can you believe it? In Egypt, the god Thoth was believed to have first introduced this concept. Halls of healing were consciously painted to introduce the specific properties of different colors to intensify healing. These days, color therapy is becoming widely accepted in modern medicine as a viable, rational form of treatment. Red light is known to benefit the treatment of wounds and cancer. Blue light is routinely used to treat jaundice in newborn infants, as well as depression and pain. In athletes, the former has been shown to amplify short bursts of energy while the latter supports sustained activity. Pink is used to subdue inmates in prisons and measurably decreases their physical strength – perhaps we should all rethink the constant pink-ness with which we surround girls if we truly want them to be strong and empowered members of society.

I have a brilliant friend whose mind works a mile a minute. He has been wearing purple lenses in his sunglasses for more than twenty years now. He says he can't bear to see the world any other way. He is prone to stress and anxiety, and works in a fast-paced technical environment. These purple lenses are actually offering him an easy source of daily stress reduction and emotional detox, even though he doesn't know anything about color therapy. It's no wonder he's come to rely on them.

To work with colors, you might choose hues that amplify or support your personality, or you might decide to use colors that balance you. If you are creative and energetic you might be drawn to green or orange – these colors will bring out your natural dynamism and creativity. If you are stressed, reach for blue; if you're angry, wear more pink. If you find yourself disliking certain colors or their combinations, it could be that you are uncomfortable with or suppressing the specific energetic traits that they express or encourage.

To really immerse yourself in a color frequency, you can paint a room a specific color or use a colored light bulb. When you add white to a color, you dampen the very aspects that it would normally encourage (hence the devitalizing effects of the color pink). When you add black to a color you lower the frequency of the color so that it is working more on a physical level than on a soul/energetic basis.

You can also drink your colors. This last method is known as **hydrochromopathy**, and does not involve food dyes. All you need for hydrochromopathy is a translucent food-safe vessel for your water and sunlight. Glass is my favorite material for holding water. Choose the color glass you want to infuse your water with, fill with good quality drinking water and place near a sunlit window for 6-8 hours. If you do not have colored glass, a clear vessel wrapped in colored paper or plastic will work just as well. Once your water has been charged you may store it in a cool dark place (the fridge is good) and drink a glass 1-5 times a day.

Here's a list of colors and what they are good for:

Brown

Stabilizing, grounding. It is calming and connects us to the earth and the root chakra, counteracting anger, overexcitement, and sexual addiction. Contraindications: rudeness, coarse behavior, infection.

Red

Warming, stimulating. Boosts confidence, ambition, and stamina. Increases sex drive and benefits blood and menstrual issues. Contraindications: impatience, irritation, anger, wounds.

Orange

Optimistic, Energizing. Social confidence and self-assurance. Benefits respiratory issues and digestion. Contraindications: irritability, over-eating, lack of inhibitions.

Yellow

Joy. The color of the Sun combats sadness and fear. Courage, decision-making, mental stimulation, inspiration. Contraindications: ADHD, superficial interactions.

Green

Induces compassion and healing. It is a general tonic for all disorders. Peace, compassion, gratitude, growth (think green thumbs). Good for heart issues. Contraindications: hyper-empathy, emotional instability, inertia.

Aqua

Cooling and calming. Helps our self-expression and find our voice. Contraindications: interrupts others, talks in monologues.

Blue

Very cooling, relaxing and anti-inflammatory. Restores the basic blueprint of the physical body. Soothes ADHD. Contraindications: depression, exhaustion, insecurity.

Indigo

Very relaxing, even sleep-inducing. Soothes anxiety and transports us to greater states of imagination. Benefits the eyes and ears. Contraindications: depression, spaced out, apathy, comas.

Violet

Recalibrates the nervous system and the energy body. Induces deep sleep states, suppresses appetite and excitement. Connects to angelic healing realms.

Contraindications: Boredom, depression, suppresses emotions.

Magenta/Pink

Soothing, relaxing. Relieve emotional burdens and aggression. Connect us with the power of prayer and angels. Contraindications: May dampen natural exuberance and full emotional range.

White

The full spectrum of visible light. Healing, strengthening and purifying, it is beneficial to virtually all conditions. Connects to Source, the spark of God-self. Contraindications: hypersensitivity, ungrounded, flighty, inactive.

Black

The absence of light, it grounds and protects us, bathing us in earth-womb energies. Use with white for significant balancing effects. Contraindications: depression, paranoia, resistance.

Ultraviolet

Antibacterial, antifungal, antiviral. Immunity boosting and healing to most systems in the body. Relieves pain and balances metabolic action. Lowers blood pressure and benefits the heart. Helps weight loss. Counteracts seasonal affective disorder and general sadness. Contraindications: skin cancer, anorexia, sunburn, vitamin D toxicity.

Let's talk a little more about the ultraviolet light and that great big lightbulb in the sky. The sun sends us a full spectrum of colors and light frequencies all day long, including ultraviolet and infrared waves which boost the immune system, help us fight illness in the body, warm us up and stimulate energy flow in the body. Although UV light can be damaging to cells in large doses (avoid sunburn, and certainly don't ever stare at the sun for any length of time!) in small, regular doses it has been shown to be quite beneficial in a variety of ways.

The fact is that we need UV light. Our bodies evolved over millennia on a planet that is bathed in sunlight every day, and our bodies adjusted to this by utilizing the sun's rays as a nutritive source of energy. Three percent of the light given off by the sun is comprised of UV rays, which are further broken down into UVA and UVB rays. We use these rays to make vitamin D and activate beneficial hormones. UV light has been shown to lower blood pressure and cholesterol, and improve heart and blood flow.

Perhaps most importantly, sunlight kills germs and bacteria, and the vitamin D production it triggers in the body has been shown to be an effective treatment or preventative for many dis-eases, including psoriasis, tuberculosis, depression, diabetes, rheumatoid arthritis, multiple sclerosis, fibromyalgia and even certain types of cancer.

Unfortunately, at least 40% of the American population is vitamin D deficient. If you are dark-skinned, your chances of being deficient double because that extra pigment blocks more UV rays. The further north you live or the more clothing you are wearing, the more time you need to spend in the sunlight you need in order to produce vitamin D and receive the healing effects of the sun. If you use sunblock, you might need to stay in the sun all day in order to process any of those UV rays around you into vitamin D. Do you drink milk with added vitamin D? Don't rely on that as your sole source, unless you are drinking 8-10 glasses a day.

NASA uses infrared and near-ultraviolet LED blankets in space to help astronauts keep their muscles strong and help injuries heal. These days, wounds, burns, bone trauma, and even cancer treatments are all the subjects of LED light therapy studies. The FDA has approved light therapy for "the relaxation of muscles and relief of muscle spasms; temporary relief of minor muscle and joint aches, pain and stiffness; temporary relief of minor pain and stiffness associated with arthritis; and to temporarily increase local blood circulation."

If all this color talk is feeling a bit too science-y for you, let's talk about something close to my heart: **art therapy**! When I was in school, I'd have good semesters and bad semesters. Months where I felt great and productive, able to handle anything the world threw at me, and months where nothing seemed to go right and just the thought of going to class was overwhelming. After a year or so of this, I realized what the trouble was with those off months. I wasn't doing any art! Sure, I had sketchbooks laying around, but school was so demanding that if I wasn't taking an art class as one of my extra-curriculars, I'd forget to spend some time expressing myself on the page. As a girl who kept a lot of emotions inside and hadn't yet discovered the power of her voice, art was a necessary outlet. Painting, sculpting, drawing, and doodling are all great ways to bring your art and mind together as a creative team and let out your emotions.

Art booking is a super fun way to wrap up each day and let off some steam. Like a bujo, an art journal is a visual diary that can become almost like a yearbook, something personal you can look back on with pride and keep for years. Also like a bujo, you can use a sketchbook, scrapbook or a composition journal for this, or you can go to the thrift shop and find a big hardcover book with nice thick pages. Each day (or week, or as often as works for you), spend 30-60 minutes making a collage, drawing or painting in your book that expresses how you are feeling. You might add inspiring words, dreams, sentences you heard that day that you're still thinking about, or things you wish you'd said. If you're painting, you might want to buy some gesso, a white paint-like medium that dries quickly. You can use this in the thrift shop book to cover the page before you start painting so that it won't warp. If you're painting thickly or gluing in lots of other papers to make collages, you might carefully cut out every other page in the book so that you have more room for your creativity.

As you go, be easy on yourself. Art booking isn't about making a showpiece to show to a gallery or teachers. It's about letting go. It's about giving yourself over to the process and immersing yourself in a world of color and texture. When you art book, you're reconnecting with your inner child, that freewheeling part of yourself that still believes that everything in the world is cool and awe-inspiring. That part of you that just wants to stick their hands in the paint and go wild. As a teen, you have probably found yourself thinking there are too many rules in the world. Your art book is a place where you get to change all that, where there are no rules, just you, the page, and your emotions.

So, let them out. Go wild. Give yourself the *space* you need to let out your dreams, your fears, your angst and silliness. Reconnect with who you really are. The more you express yourself in safe and creative ways, the more relaxed you'll be. It might seem crazy, but something as simple as art booking can be the ticket to a more comfortable, fulfilling life. Give it a try!

It's Elemental

If you study with any sort of spirituality for any length of time, eventually you will encounter references to the elements. These do not refer just to the elements of weather but also to the elements within the body. The elements have their roots in the very birth of life energy modalities: vitalism. The concept of vitalism is central to most systems of indigenous healing, as well as newer biofield therapies: Ayurveda, Reiki, Shamanism, Traditional Chinese Medicine (TCM), and Polarity Therapy all work around the basic premise that the proper function of the body itself is contingent upon the healthy flow of a vital life force. You can also call this vital force Qi, Prana or Source Energy.

Most systems that center on vitalism discuss the importance of harmonizing the elements within the body. When the elements are out of balance meridians become blocked, agitated or sluggish; chakras shut down; biological functions suffer. In general, there are between 3 and 5 elements addressed by most systems. For our purposes here, we will address the five most commonly discussed in the Western Hemisphere: Earth, Air, Fire, Water, and Ether.

The **earth** element is generally associated with the north and dark, earthy colors: black, red, brown. Green evokes the life-giving energy of the earth element. When someone is out of balance with the earth element they will often be described as flighty, spacey or hyperactive. They might suffer from joint and muscle pain, be stubborn, overly cautious or fearful. Feel like you have rocks in your shoulders? Maybe your muscles are trying to remind you to connect to the earth element.

What happens if you're not connected to the earth element? Your life may begin to feel meaningless and undirected, or you might start daydreaming a lot or be worried about your ability to take care of yourself. That's where grounding comes in. When you are grounded, the energy of Source can flow through you at optimum levels improving your physical incarnation – your body and your reality – here on Earth. Massage your pinkies to help ground excess energy in your body.

Air is the element that connects our thoughts and minds, it is the natural element that directs our individual connection to mass consciousness, to the living, conscious earth matrix of all beings. In our body, it is centered in our chest and our lungs and affects our ability to expand and truly live. It is literally the breath of life, but it often goes unnoticed by many of us, despite the fact that it is so important to us for our minute-to-minute survival. It is associated most often with the color yellow, the direction east, the sunrise, and new beginnings. This is appropriate because Air tends to bring us new ideas. Air governs the mind, our motivation, and intellect. When our air element is balanced, we feel free and easy. We flow with life in a relaxed yet productive way.

If you are deficient in air you might feel tired or detached. Without air, it is difficult for us to move, physically and energetically. Your upper back will tighten and lock up, your chest will constrict and you will find it hard to feel motivated or connected to life. If you have an over-abundance of air, you might have too many ideas and not know where to start, or you might feel rushed and be moving too quickly. The best way to connect with the air element is through breath work or singing. Playing the flute or any other wind instrument, especially outside, is also very helpful. In the body, the air element is connected to the index fingers and second toes – massaging either of these can activate and normalize the flow of air throughout the body.

On a nice day, you might try standing outside with very little clothing on and raising your arms to the winds. This exercise can be a very simple and effective way to begin feeling and connecting to the air spirits. Many people resonate with one specific directional wind. The North wind is cold, serious, honest and pure. The East wind comes most often as a playful breeze, young and easy. The South wind blows warm and comforting, but also full of passion and has a fiery temper. The West wind can be both wise and melancholy. If you are interested in working with the winds, get to know them personally and see who complements your personality the best, and who might be your best ally or teacher.

Burning incense or smudging with herbs like sage, mugwort or cedar also connects us to the element of air, because smoke travels on the wind to carry our prayers to spirit. Says Mic-mac shaman and elder, Evan Pritchard:

"[Smudges like] the sweetgrass and cedar are not only medicine, they each embody the four elements. The earth womb they grew from, the water that nourished them, the sun-fire that enlivened them, and the air they breathe – all four elements. To burn them while smudging is to change them from a sleeping to an active state. The smoke embodies the prayers of the people as it rises to heaven."

Fire is powerful, coming to us from the center of the earth, from the south if you are in the Northern Hemisphere, as both a creative and destructive force. It is a transmuting element, changing the form of everything it touches. Fire is a good element to work with when you are trying to add energy or power to your spiritual work. Candles are used in religious rituals worldwide for this very reason. They light a spark against the dark, so that we may clearly see the way. In northern cultures especially, the tribal fire-keeper was always respected and trusted, someone with authority and power. They made sure there was always an ember available to kindle other fires, so that no one in the tribe would ever be cold or lack a cooking fire. They were friends with the air spirits and the plants, because a good fire required knowledge of what to burn and how to safely feed the fire.

In the body, fire manifests as Qi and Kundalini energy, where its warmth and strength creates movement and stimulation. Without internal heat fire, we cannot move our bodies and eliminate food waste. Fire creates action and impulse in the mind. Fiery people are quick to act and react, full of energy, and generally dashing about from activity to activity. "She's on fire" or "they're fired up" are phrases we are familiar with. When fire is unbalanced, anger can flare ("he's got a fiery personality" can be a mild way of saying that someone is quick to anger). Not surprisingly, on the hands and feet, fire rules the middle digit, so a little massaging of that finger can help douse your ire.

What should we do when fire flares? If you suppress it and ignore it, you will create a dormant anger, much like a volcano, that creates toxicity in the body and in relationships. When it finally blows, you'll feel depleted and guilty, suddenly devoid of fire and energy. So what to do? Allow it to be. Express it physically with exercise or a safe activity. Write it down. Talk it out. Let it out gently and freely, but not by acting in a fiery, impulsive way. Remember that we need fire. Fire is Sun energy – without it, our body goes cold and locks up. Our emotions can become too watery or heavy. Fire helps lighten the load, when used and expressed properly. It gives us the energy we need to birth the reality we conceive of.

Water, the very opposite of fire, makes up more of our physical form than any of the other four elements. We will die faster if we go without water than without food, although our culture tends to be much more concerned with hunger than thirst. Humanity's evolutionary migration out of Africa is believed to have been sparked by drought, driving our ancestors out of the suddenly arid lands in search of more plentiful sources of water and food. Indeed, until the modern era of large ships, water was the boundary of all land. People did not look at the seas and large rivers as areas of no consequence between communities and nations. Even cultures that had boats, like the Phoenicians and the Vikings, maintained a healthy fear of the water. The seas could be calm and gentle, then turn cold, stormy and unpredictable in a matter of minutes.

Water as an element in most healing traditions relates to emotion, sexuality, creativity, the processing and elimination of toxins and blood. In the chakras, it can be found most abundantly in the second chakra. It is generally associated with the color blue, as well as the color orange in some traditions (which makes sense when one remembers that the second chakra is generally orange.) Since the sun sets in the west and water relates to elimination and emotions, it is not surprising that in many traditions it, along with the underworld, is linked with the west.

If the water element is unbalanced, the person will be too! Empathic people often have too much water going on, and really need to work on balancing this element since too much water results in an overabundance of emotion, often accompanied by crying, sadness, or depression. Physically the person may manifest water weight, fungal infections, reproductive issues, sweats or elimination problems. Too little water generally results in an overabundance of fire, making people feel brittle and over-stimulated. Water can be balanced by massaging your ring finger — the same finger many cultures wear their wedding bands on to ensure our emotions do not stray.

Finally, we come to the fifth element. **Ether** is present in all spiritual traditions and goes by many names. Qi. Orenda. Spirit. Aether. Akasha. Source Energy. Quintessence. In the Wiccan tradition, it is shown at the top of the five-pointed star – the element that energizes and enlivens the other five. In most Native American traditions, it is at the center of the four directions, above and below us, within us and around us. In Eastern traditions, it is everywhere: the animating, unifying principle of Qi or Spirit that moves us all.

When ether is balanced in a person, they feel peaceful and confident. They are connected to Source and their higher selves. Early indications of an ether imbalance include a lack of self-confidence; stress and anxiety; hearing and balance issues; vertigo; joint problems; introspection, depression or non-communication; a lack of boundaries or feeling hemmed in. You can help balance your ether element by massaging your thumbs — the largest digit for the most important of elements! Remember, if ether is out of balance in the body, all other elements will suffer and decline. You'll be tired, and eventually quite sick as the elemental centers begin to shut down. Without ether, there is nothing. No life. No Spirit. No divinity. Nothing. Ether is indeed quintessential. It is the non-physical energy out of which all life and matter on earth spring forth. Think of ether as the quantum space between atoms and particles, the space that goes on forever, with no real physicality to it except that which we have all agreed to see and feel.

Remember, if you want to keep all your elements balanced, an easy thing to do is to massage your feet or hands, paying special attention to each of your fingers or toes.

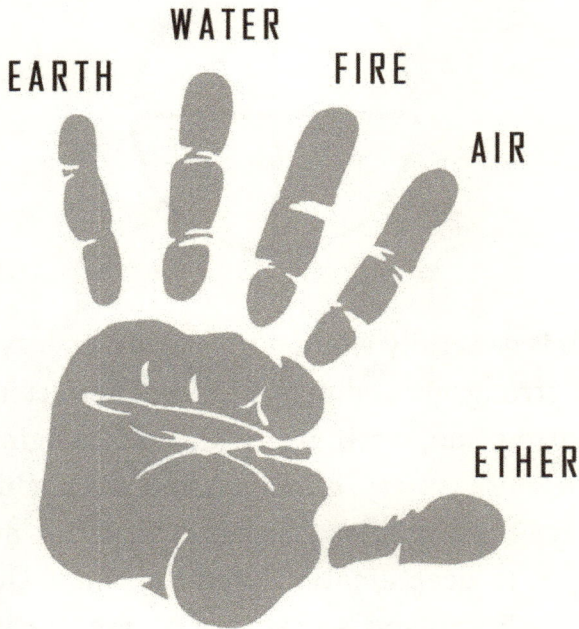

EARTH   WATER   FIRE   AIR   ETHER

Another good way to keep yourself aligned is to work with the **medicine wheel**. Directions have always had a major role in every culture around the world, and medicine wheels or sacred hoops can be found in most indigenous, tribal communities. The medicine wheel is built like the compass, having a center with four cardinal arms, like spokes, which when connected form a wheel. It is not surprising that we have wound up with four primary directions. We ourselves are comprised of a right and a left, a front and a back. The medicine wheel is a compass not only for our external world, but also for our own internal reality. The cross is simply one more adaptation of this representation.

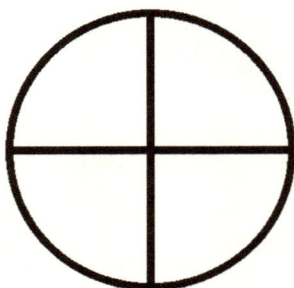

The North is generally aligned with Earth energy, mountain energy. It is strong, grounding, and wise. The East is associated with the rising sun, with fresh air, new beginnings, and change. The South is fiery, full of passion and excitement. The West is where the sun sets, it brings completion and healing, connecting us to deep emotions and the water element. The center of the wheel is you, and you, of course, are Spirit. When you are balanced and connected, you are one with Spirit, you are one with everything. You are one with the wheel of life. Source energy flows easily through you and around you. You are one with your higher purpose and you can walk your true path, the one with a heart.

Medicine wheels vary widely between tribes and cultures. Some use different colors for different directions, some have up to 28 spokes (perhaps representing lunar cycles), and some are 75 feet across! In the Northern US, the most common wheel colors used are red, white, yellow and black. These four colors create a wheel that represents not only the four directions, but also the four tribes of humans on the earth as portrayed in most Native American creation myths.

You can work with medicine wheels simply by making one out of rocks on your dresser or outside in the woods, or you can draw one and hang it up in your room as a visual reminder to stay in balance. Remember — you are the center of your wheel, always standing at the center of your world and reality. What's in each of your directions that balances you? What can you do that you enjoy to harmonize your water, temper your fire, breathe fresh life into your air, or ground your earth? Here's a meditation you can use to connect with the four directions: mayacointreau.com/transform/fourelements.mp3

The Seat of the Four Elements

To begin this meditation, you take four deep breaths.

Breathe in. Breathe out.

Breathe in. Breathe out.

Breathe in. Breathe out.

Breathe in. Breathe out.

With each breath go deeper within your body, down into your inner point of stillness. Here within your self is a still point, a quiet darkness where creation begins. Here, anything is possible.

You are a god within your own body.

In the darkness, you rise up, and begin to walk a spiral path away from where you sat. Your way is lit in the darkness by small crystals twinkling beneath your feet, as if you are a giant walking along the Milky Way.

Feel your energy expand as spiral outward, the energy of the star crystals flowing up through your feet, up into your body. From your toes, up to your knees, through your thighs, into your solar plexus, and radiating up and outward through your heart, head and hands.

See yourself glowing in the darkness as you walk the path, your body is radiant, light and energy.

Your light shines on the earth below you, part of the night sky above a mountain range. The tallest mountain, covered with snow, calls to you, and you use stars as your stepping stones to reach the mountain peak.

Here, you stand, and take in the cool mountain air. The wind whispers in your ear, playing with your hair, and welcomes you to the Seat of the Four Elements.

The wind gently twirls and pushes you, until you face South. The air from this direction blows hotter, and you see a mountain blowing fire and ash into the sky. The element of Fire rises to greet you, and the first light of dawn casts a warm, red glow all around you.

You feel the warmth radiate through your body, infusing you with renewed vitality. Any negative energy that has been stored in your body is consumed and transformed into renewed life-force pulsing within you. Visualize the flames chasing away any darkness within and without you, protecting you from darkness here, now, in the past, and in the future.

Now see these gentle flames settle down, flowing along your bloodlines, becoming part of you, forever burning off infections and renewing depleted energy sources. The element of Fire is part of your birthright as a human being, and you can call upon it whenever you need it.

On the mountaintop, the wind gently spins you again, and now you face West, a vast ocean before you. A fresh, clear breeze comes in off the water, carrying with it water and vapor, and you welcome the Element of Water. When you close your eyes you can feel the spray of the ocean against your face, and a warm, quiet rain begins to fall around you.

Water has come to cleanse your emotions and fill your soul. Water carries the power of intuition with it, the ability to feel emotions with the body and bring the fire of creation into the physical. Your body is made almost entirely of water, reacts strongly to the purity of water around it.

You open your eyes, and see a shell before, filled with clear, cool, perfect water. You hold it in your two hands, and send it thoughts of love and compassion. As you drink the water, feel the love and compassion flow back into you, down your throat, into your belly, infusing your entire body with love.

In our Oceans, Compassion is the energy that sends the tides our, and Love is the vibration that keeps the tides flowing in. The water in our bodies also responds to Love and

Compassion, feel them flowing in and out of you as you breathe, a never-ending cycle of perfect trust.

As you continue breathing, the wind begins again to blow, and gently buffets you to face North. Mountains stretch as far as the eye can see, covered with deep green forests and peaks capped with snow. Streams winding down the mountainsides become wider, deeper rivers that wind around the bases of the mountains. These mountains have been here forever, it seems, and though they have been molded by wind, fire and water, they have stood the test of time.

The element of Earth greets you as the smell of freshly dug earth travels on the breeze, and the day grows brighter, the sun a clear yellow above the horizon on your right. The earth trembles slightly underneath your feet, reminding you that the mountain you stand on was born of lava, the creative side of the Earth element.

You close your eyes as the earth continues to tremble, gently, yet you feel reassurance, and the promise of strength flowing up through the sole of your feet. Earth is here to carry you. It carries you through life, through death, and through every moment. For protection and comfort, you can turn to the earth. When you feel weak, you can turn to the earth for strength.

Imagine roots growing from the tips of your toes, from the heels of your feet, from the center of your soles. These roots grow deep into the ground, feeding you, nourishing you, and re-energizing you. Like a Banyan tree, you can send roots from your fingertips, your arms, from along your spine, to root in the Earth, feed your spirit and heal your body. Feel the life-force of the Universe flow up the roots you have grown and into you, pulsing through your veins, your organs, your skin and your hair.

When you have finished, draw your roots back into your body, stored within you for future use. The Earth is here to help you whenever you ask. In return, you feed her with the breath of life.

As you breathe in and out, enjoying your new energy levels, the wind surrounds you, blowing harder, and spins you to the East. By now the sun is high overhead, and clouds race by, carried on the Wind.

The Element of Air whispers around you, quietly, in many voices, carrying knowledge and wisdom. Spirit soars on the wind, and your soul lifts within you as you listen to the air rush around you.

Your higher self talks to you through the wind. You feel your crown chakra open, and the will of The Great Spirit, your Higher Self, and the Divine pour into you, carried on a gentle conduit of Air. Feel the breath of life flow through you, expanding your lungs, your diaphragm, your belly, giving fresh oxygen to every cell in your body.

Air is life-sustaining, and carries the secret of immortality.

Breathe in the fresh air, and feel old cells regenerating, rebuilding, and casting off damage at a molecular level.

Continue breathing, and imagine the Wind teaching your body to do this on its own, to remember the breath of Life, and to use it for healing and regeneration forever and ever.

Feel your self seated on the peak of this mountain, radiant and whole. Feel your spirit, not above you or separate, but filling you up, and flowing out from you in all directions. YOU are the fifth direction, the fifth element, Spirit. Without spirit, the four elements have no guide, and cannot connect. Within you, the four elements harmonize, and balance.

Feel the health and Fire of creation flowing through your veins, the purity of Water cleansing you, the protection and power of Earth fueling you, and the Breath of Life surrounding you, as Air blows in, and out.

Breathe the elements in, and out. In, and out.

When you are ready, return.

Getting Outside and Getting in Touch

Fields of grain to feed us. Forests of trees acting as the lungs of the world. Oceans for cleansing, birdsong to lift our hearts, sweet berries and fruits to bring smiles to our faces. The earth is our playground, our mother and home. It takes care of us and can offer solace when nothing else will. When life is less than satisfying, get outside and spend some time in nature grounding yourself, soaking up negative ions, and letting the winds carry your worries away.

Take a walk and find a stone to hold in your hand, rubbing it as you go, or find a large rock to sit or lean on. Many indigenous creation legends tell us about the souls and personalities of rocks. The old stories tell us that **the stone people** were here before the plants, the root-people. They were here before the four-leggeds and the bird people. They were here before us. The stone people are the record-keepers. They have incredibly long memories, both geologic and historical. They know our histories and other the stories from before we came to be. They move ever so slowly, but they hold exceptionally high vibrations and amounts of information.

They can't come to us on our own, but they will have ways to travel to where we will find them – trout might carry a stone upstream, where raccoon gathers it and brings it to an elemental, who will then throw it at your feet, just before the moment you look down to mind your steps and think, *hmm, what a nice rock*, and stick it in your pocket. When you buy a stone in a shop, think about all the work it has done to be in just the right place, at the right time, so that it could make its way to you!

Crystals can be used singly or in groups. You can use a single stone to meditate with or hold while you sleep to enhance visions and dreaming. You can place them on the body to amplify the flow of energy between the chakras or meridians, or to heal a specific area or blockages. Different crystals have different uses, just like different families of herbs. And specific crystals (plants, too!) within each family have their own personality – just like you may share many traits with your own relatives, but are also unique in your own personality.

Different crystal shapes can affect the way the power of the crystal works. When you use a totally raw, unshaped stone straight from a mine or picked up off the ground, you are working with the pure power of the stone, whatever that might be. Tumbled stones have a gentler energy, and send their power out to whoever rubs them awake – they tend to go relatively dormant during the tumbling process, so you might need to wake them up again by rubbing them or talking to them. Faceted or cut gemstones and crystal points have precisely directed, amplified energy that beams from their points or apexed faces. Crystal wands or rods are especially good for directing crystalline energy. Sometimes you will see wands that have one round end and one pointed end. The round end can be used to massage trigger points on the body and direct tension away from the away, while the pointy end can be used to direct the stone's energy to a specific point. Pyramids and obelisks (pointed standing towers) can be used to amplify and generate energy and are great for creating domes of protection or increased energy for manifestation, while crystal balls tend to emit a gentle energy in all directions.

You can use crystals to shift the energy in your house, your room, or even the earth by placing them strategically on certain energy points or gridding them around your living spaces. I love putting a small rose quartz in each corner of my bedroom to help the room feel cozy, loving and protected. Four pieces of black tourmaline to anchor each corner of the house will help shield it from lower frequencies, and selenite gridded around a home will clear everybody's energy, helping keep things calm and relaxed. If you feel like there's a part of the house, property or neighborhood that is "off", a place where people get sad, angry, or nervous more than other spaces, chances are there is some geopathic stress going and the energy system of the earth itself needs to be balanced there. Just as Qi runs through our chakras and meridians, so it does on the earth. Sometimes, these power points and meridians, called ley lines, get disturbed or blocked up, just like ours. This is a problem, since ley lines are the gridwork that affirms and maintains the integrity of our physical dimension.

Ley lines are the earth's living matrix, and comprise all the information, vibration and emotions of all beings on earth, as well as the blueprint for the earth herself. Most people cannot see ley lines, but many of those who can report their appearance as a brilliant blue gridwork over the ground. Some see them as a white haze, much the same way people view the etheric aspect of the aura around the body. Ley lines can be very thin or very wide – inches or miles! If you can balance some of the ley lines in your area, that positive energy will help the rest of the planet be healthier — humans too.

Pendulums can be used to **dowse** for water, ley lines, mineral deposits and more. To check your home or local ley lines for geopathic stress, first find the ley lines: ask your pendulum which way it will swing when it crosses a ley line or an area of geopathic stress, then walk around slowly until you get a hit. Once you've found one, ask its permission to work with them with a yes or no answered by pendulum or sway testing. Then, you can determine if the area or ley line is distorted, healthy or dormant/drained. Singing bowls or drums may be used to re-energize ley lines and clear geopathic distortions, or you can spend some time moaning and toning to clear and heal the energy flow, followed by some transfigurational toning to really wake it up and get it moving in a positive manner for everybody's highest good.

If you want to work even more with the natural energies around your home or in the wild, think about connecting with the **elementals**. What are they, and how can they help? Some other names for these spiritual creatures are nature devas, fairies, little people, the fair folk, and nature spirits. There are lots of different kinds, but the thing their main defining feature is that they are highly conscious beings who reside on our planet in non-physical form. Some of them (fairies, gnomes, sprites) help nature do its thing, encouraging plants to grow and protecting natural, wild spots. Some of them (devas, overlighting angels) are actually associated with the spirit of a particular plant family or area.

All of them tend to get excited when a new human can sense them—once you start talking to them you'll probably find it hard not to notice them. They are eager to co-create with us, to share their ideas and messages with us. They want nothing more than to help us help ourselves. They wish only for the world to be harmonious and beautiful. They want all beings, all animals, plants, people, stones — everything on earth — to be in balance. Sometimes they might seem angry or proud, or a little wild and scary. That's nature!

Fairies and gnomes began as regular physical entities, much like us. They were slightly higher in vibration, slightly less physical, but they were here on earth. Eventually, they progressed to a point where they were yearning to work more with the energies that support physical life, more with the spiritual energies of love behind the plants, and less with the flowers or trees themselves. They reside now in a vastly different plane of existence where all is energy and physical rules as we know them do not apply. Having been of our physical realm, they can still connect with us when it is necessary or wanted, but they can also connect more easily with Source energy.

Devas create magic with the physical manifestations of the land and the earth. They are purely non-physical beings. They play with the wind and the trees, the skies and the waters. Devas are more intimately involved in the workings of the nature of the earth. Devas have also been called nature spirits, daikinis, sprites and sylphs over the years and you can find stories about them in every culture on Earth. Each location on the planet, every little stream, each field, each flower species, every breeze has its own deva, its own spirit, complete with its own independent personality and disposition.

Overlighting angels are the angelic beings that work specifically with the Earth itself. They are in a different business than the archangels you might have heard of – Michael, Raphael, Gabriel, Uriel. Those guys watch over humanity. Overlighting angels watch over Gaia. The overlighting angels are more removed from us than devas. They watch, and they help channel energy to the areas they watch. They speak with the devas and fairies, and feel empathy for all living creatures in their area but they do not intervene on a physical level as much as the fae. They can and do help devas and humans clear negative energy from areas when they are called in, and they do help connect humanity to Source. But they do not shift the winds or the rains or the sun or make the plants grow swifter or taller. That is the work and the play of the devas, the cloud people and the fairies.

Every piece of earth has an overlighting angel. Some watch small areas of earth, and some watch very large pieces of earth. Most pieces of earth have several overlighting angels watching over them, at different levels, feeling different stages of connection and inter-personal connectedness. So your home or street has an overlighting angel, as well as your city, the general area of your state, and the area of your country, and also your entire continent. The overlighting Angels often use different boundaries than our ever-shifting human maps, but you get the idea. Our entire planet has an overlighting angel called the Sun.

Angels and fairies can be called upon to help better connect you to the earth or other elements of nature such as the sun, moon, plants or animals. They are particularly attuned to clearing spaces, large or small, just call on the right one for the job. An overlighting angel can clear big areas of geopathic stress or energetic disturbances in mass consciousness. Local devas are wonderful for helping re-energize ley lines that have become corrupted or disturbed. Think about the size of space you want to clean, and then call in the appropriate nature spirit(s). Always ask them respectfully for their help. They do not appreciate being ordered around, but are eager to assist us in any way they can, so long as our motives and our intentions are pure. Be as clear as you can about what you would like them to do, and within minutes, days or weeks, depending on the job you set them to, you will see definite improvements. Ask if there is anything you can do in return or addition to what they are doing: you may be asked to put a specific crystal somewhere or plant something outside. Often, fairies respond with a request that you do some greening up in a park or let a small portion of your land grow wild for a season. Even if you do not hear the fairies or the angels speak to you, trust that they are there, and they do hear your requests. If they do not ask you for anything in return, a heartfelt "Thank you" is always appreciated when you are finished. Joyfully, lovingly, for their hearts are pure, they seek to help humanity heal itself and heal the planet around them. Remember to approach the devas with respect and love in your heart, and they will respond in kind.

Your Spirit Tribe

When you work with spirit, spirit rises to work with you. Source is always seeking to support you, and the more you practice the techniques in this book, the more you'll begin to have different spiritual mentors appear in your life. At school, you might connect with a special teacher just when you most need some advice you can respect. In your meditations or dreams, you might start to be visited by animals or people who keep you company or give you guidance on your travels. These non-physical spiritual mentors come by many names including power animals, clan totems, spirit guides, ascended masters and soul groups. What's the difference and what do they do? Well, let's see.

Power animals are animal archetypes or over-souls that join us in our spirit work. When we meditate, we might find ourselves walking with a jaguar across mountaintops or following a squirrel to a beautiful lake. You might even find yourself connecting with a beloved pet, living or alive. Animals are less bogged down by fear and worries, and more connected to Source energy in many ways. They take each day as it comes and can be wonderful teachers. In the spirit realm, they fear nothing and know everything — where to go to find peace, what cave has all the tools you need to work on healing your body, who to see to help relieve some of your burdens. Each power animal taps into the archetypal aspects of its species, as well as its own personality. Some are quiet and serious; some make jokes and will talk through your entire meditation. Power animals often show up first in our dreams. Big cats might prowl around your home or wolves might chase you across fields, which can seem a little nerve-wracking but they're just trying to say hello. You might keep seeing images of an animal in magazine or TV ads, or plastered on billboards trying to get your attention. Power animals don't have to be things you'd find in a zoo, either — I've met people with unicorns, pterodactyls and saber-toothed tigers as guides!

If you have a specific animal that you've always been drawn to, that might be a guide, but it could also be a **clan totem**. Everybody has some clan totems, though they probably don't know it. Entire groups of Viking berserkers connected strongly to wolf and bear energies and would wear the animal pelts into battle, taking on the fierceness of their totems (berserk literally meant "bear shirt"). They were nearly unstoppable. Clan totems weren't just for fighting: there were turtle people, owl tribes, horse clans — all sorts of familial and tribal groups from all over the world who connected with a particular animal energetic generation after generation. If you're a human, you have a clan totem somewhere in your past, waiting for you to call it into service. These clan totems are your birthright, a part of your DNA. Connect to yours and know that it is always there for extra support or protection, whenever you need an ally.

Spirit guides are similar to power animals, but they can be anything. You might have a wise ancestor, an angel, an old medicine woman, or a disembodied ball of loving energy as a spirit guide. Spirit guides can come in all forms. Like power animals, they are here to assist you with healing and offer guidance.

Where power animals tend to travel with us from place to place throughout our dreams and meditations, going everywhere with us and acting as trail guides, most spirit guides tend to remain in certain areas, waiting for us to come to them or to call them to us.

Ascended masters are high-level guides who used to live here on earth, did pretty great things, and entered the angelic realms after they died or ascended. Historic figures like Jesus, Buddha, Mary Magdalene, Saint Germaine, Metatron, and Kwan Yin are all considered Ascended Masters. They are like regular guides, but since they did pretty well on earth spiritually, their advice is often considered a little more helpful. In fact, if you find that your guides aren't giving you great advice, fire them! You can always ask for new guides that fit your goals better. Some people like to make sure that all their guides have recently spent time here on earth in physical bodies, because otherwise how can they really understand what you are going through? If you want to do great in business, you might ask to talk with a Rockefeller or Napoleon Hill. If you want to be a baker, maybe Julia Child will have some advice for you. When you're meditating or doing spiritual work, don't be afraid to think outside the box: there is no box!

Soul groups are not single guides, but collectives of consciousness that can offer us lots of support. All souls have core groups that they are linked to, collectives of other souls working towards similar goals, sort of like classes you might be part of at school or a sports club. Just like these the kids in real-world groups, these souls can move between groups, and share groups, so you can have special soul-connections with lots of different types of people. Imagine if you were to draw three circles, all overlapping in the middle. You can connect with many different soul groups, though not everyone from one group might feel connected with the people from another group.

When you are with someone of the same soul group, they are more likely to remain your friend or in your life, despite any differences you might have over the years. They will enjoy being in your presence and feel a slight boost to their own vibration when they are. This is normal for people in the same soul group. Soul mates are really just people from your soul group(s) — meeting one does not mean that you need to be together romantically or have a close friendship. It can be beneficial to have even one conversation, because when you talk or sit with a person in your soul group it helps awaken your spirit. Thus, being near members of your soul group(s) helps you heal more quickly, identify your path more easily, and receive guidance from your higher self more clearly. In many ways, you can be each other's muse, their inspiration. You are good for each other — usually.

Sometimes, soul group connections can be so intense or pleasurable that they are mistaken for romantic connection (and sometimes they are that). There is a strong sense of joy connected to being with one's soul group. It is a feeling of home. This is why it is important to be clear about what your feelings are, and where they come from. You will feel a strong, similar connection whenever you meet someone from your soul group. They may even feel like a soul mate, though it might just be the feelings of old lifetimes and connections bleeding through into your current reality (we'll talk more about those later). For this reason when you first meet a new person whom you are feeling this soul-connection to, we suggest that you perform a little meditation or simply state your intent quietly and firmly to yourself: I *clear and remove any all karmic ties or debris that is connected to myself and _____, and clear any past, present and future lives that might be affecting this current relationship.*"

Once such a clearing is requested, then you may embark on a fresh relationship without any old baggage getting in the way, or any old programs being repeated. After all, who needs repeats? This life is for creation and joy, a time for new expression. Free yourself and enjoy your time wherever you are.

So, are you ready to **access your own guides**? Here's a simple meditation you can do to meet one. Once you've connected with a guide, move on to the next chapter and we'll explore some more ways you can work together. www.mayacointreau.com/transform/guidance.mp3.

The Temple of Guidance

To begin this meditation, you take three deep breaths.

Breathe in. Breathe out.

Breathe in. Breathe out.

Breathe in. Breathe out.

Let your tensions go as you breathe out. Release all the stress you've accumulated over the week.

Breathe in. Breathe out.

Breathe in. Breathe out.

Breathe in. Breathe out.

Feel yourself relax. Let go.

When you breathe in, feel the purity of the air cleanse you, clear you. You are a clear vessel, hollow, clean, pure.

Feel yourself fill with peace, with calmness.

With each breath go deeper within your body, deeper, and deeper. All around you, the air is still, clear, pure. You go deeper, and deeper into the darkness of creation.

Let yourself go.

Breathe in. Breathe out.

In the darkness, you rise up, and begin to walk west, into the night. Stars glimmer before you, above you. The ground is sandy and soft beneath your bare feet. In the distance, you hear the sound of the ocean.

You continue walking west, towards the sound of the waves. You climb over and between small sand dunes, enjoying the feel of the sand beneath your feet.

The moon emerges from behind the clouds and lights your way. You see the ocean before you, the moon reflecting on its vast surface. Between the beach and the dunes, there are many large rocks, and you walk among them. Some of the rocks tower above you, solid, and strong.

One set of stones is stacked upon itself, a small building made of five huge flat stones. Each side is a large stone, and the roof is a flat stone laid upon the others. There are spaces between the stones so that it is easy to enter into the stone building, and you walk inside.

Here you have come to the Temple of Guidance. You touch the rock walls, feel them smooth in some places, rough in others. Patches of moss and lichen grow in the crevices.

The Temple of Guidance bridges the astral, shamanic and etheric planes and our dimension. It allows our guides from the light to communicate directly with us, when we may have had a hard time hearing them in the past. We have come here today so that you may meet one or more of your guides. Guides have many purposes, some teach us the way to wisdom and evolution, some are healers, some help us open up to our fullest potential. Some are here to literally guide us when we dream, journey and meditate so that we never lose our way. A guide may be your higher self, a deceased relative or friend, a power animal, a being from another realm or dimension. A guide may be the wind, the thunder or the rain. It may have many forms, or none at all. Do not be afraid. Here you are safe, and any guide that comes through may have only your higher purpose and good in mind.

As you place your hands on the stones around you, call out to your guides. Announce yourself, and state your intentions. See your guide enter the temple. Introduce yourselves, and know that you can always find each other here again.

Your guide may take you places, or you may stay here and work together. Trust yourself, and trust your guide, and let yourself be led on this journey with love and trust. When it is time to return, thank your guide, run back through the dunes, into your world and return to your body.

Old Ways for New Times

A person sets up a sacred circle on a mountaintop, gets ready to pray and call on Source for peace in their community. They need wisdom. They need guidance. They know they can't do it all on their own. They call out to their ancestors and begin to pray as the full moon rises over distant hills.

When Native Americans say the words "all my ancestors" in prayer, they don't just refer to their family, but also to the previous worlds and races of men that came before them, to all the animals, stones and beings we discussed in the last chapter. Medicine women, shamans, and lightworkers throughout history have worked with these ancestors and the realms of Spirit, with Energy, to benefit their communities, for their family, their circle of friends, their village, country or the planet. This has been the primary charge of shamans in every culture since time immemorial. Lightworkers and shamans understand the interconnectedness of all things, all beings, and strive to create a more harmonious, light-based realm on Earth.

Over the last several centuries human populations have grown while shamans have decreased, creating an imbalance in the world. You can help restore that balance by becoming comfortable in your own skin and working to improve the world around you. Each small act of balance shifts the web of humanity and helps to create a better world.

Shamans around the world have long used drums, rattles, song, and dance to quickly reach deep trance states. Scientific studies have shown that repetitive heartbeat style drumming quickly shifts brain waves to a deep meditative dream state that resonates with the same frequency as the earth itself. When we drum, we dream, and we are in full vibrational alignment with the earth's living matrix. When this happens, we come into alignment with our birth purpose, with our soul's intentions and the most positive wishes of mass consciousness.

Shamanic journeying is easier for most people than meditating. Basically, it is like being in a guided meditation, except the only guide is your spirit and the drum. When you journey, you aren't turning off your thoughts – you are freeing them, enhancing them. Drums and rattles quell our ego and relax our body, allowing our inner self to soar freely into the realms of spirit. It is here that we can gain insight, wisdom, healing and guidance, right from Spirit. If you have a drum or a rattle, practice drumming yourself into meditation. You can use anything for this — a can with some beans or rice in it, a plastic container with the lid on — you don't need to have a fancy drum to journey. For your first journey, I recommend listening to this introductory meditation and drumming at: www.mayacointreau.com/transform/firstjourney.mp3.

When you drum, no fancy skills are needed, just maintain a steady, regular rhythm that reminds you of the beats of your feet hitting the ground while you walk – it is this rhythm that will help keep you on track during your travels. A good length of time to spend on your journey is somewhere between 10-30 minutes – if you are drumming yourself, simply return when you feel complete. If you are drumming for someone other than yourself, you will need to add what is called a "call back" to the end of the journey. A call back lets people know that it is time to thank their guides and return swiftly back into their bodies. This is achieved by hitting the drum slowly four times and then hitting the drum double-time for 30-60 seconds, as if the foot-beats are now running, followed by a final four, slow beats to signal the journey's end. You can also listen to my own drumming track with rattles and rainsticks at www.mayacointreau.com/transform/drumming.mp3.

If you did the meditation in the last chapter, then you've already met your first guide. Shamans always work with power animals or spirit guides. The more work you do in the shamanic realms (or indeed, with any sort of spiritual, meditative or healing work), the more guides you are likely to meet. Each guide is different and can help you with different things. Some guides will help you travel quickly through dark realms or find lost things. Some guides will teach you to fly or swim. Some are adept at healing and will teach you their special methods. Some will help you find your voice; some know how to dance through time and space. The best guides know how to navigate through all domains of Mother Earth.

The most important thing is to remember that teachers come in all forms and sizes.

As you learn to journey it's easiest to have a private, special **place of power** that you can always start from, a place where you know your power animals and guides will always be ready to meet you, a place that fills your heart with joy and excites you. To begin, let's embark on a journey to discover what this perfect place is for you. It might be a real location that you've been to many times or somewhere you read about in a book. It might be a place you've never imagined, or it might be your own backyard. It might be a temple in Asia, some standing stones in Europe, a field in Kansas or a dock by a lake. It might be a desert cave or a jungle forest. The more you journey, the more places you will collect. I have many places I journey from, depending on where I'm planning to go, just as I have many guides that work with me, depending on what our focus is that day. But we all have a special place that will always be our first gathering point, our first power spot that holds a special place in our heart. When you have some quiet time set aside, start drumming or listen to my drumming track and do a little journey to find yours. Imagine yourself in this cozy wild place and take time to explore. You might want to sit quietly in the space and meditate, getting comfortable with its energy. Call out for your guides to join you and ask if they have any messages for you. Enjoy this time, become comfortable in your space and the journey realm.

Try to journey every week, getting to know guides that can take you into the sky, up to the moon, into your body, to healing caves and places that make your heart soar. You can perform journeys to help other people or even work on healing your own physical body, which we'll talk about more in the next chapter.

Your body and your aura are constantly interacting with the energy of the "external" world. You exchange energy with everything is that around you, whether you mean to or not. This is simply a matter of physics. All energy is connected and interactive. Connecting is part of the web of life. However, while we were designed to enjoy the ebb and flow of energy around us, we were also designed to receive our sustaining energy through our connection with Source and the Earth. As humanity has become further and further removed from Spirit, people have learned to soak up other sources of energy. Rather than connecting with Source, which will sustain us with pure, high vibration energy, many people mistake the joy of connection to other people for a good source of sustaining energy. It has become commonplace for humans to gather portions of their energy, their etheric energy, from other people. People do this with family, loved ones, friends, and even enemies. Energy exchanges can feel good, but they can also lead to co-dependence and power plays in relationships.

When we exchange energy with other people, sometimes we form **cords of attachment**. These cords might form on unintentionally, or on purpose. They are designed to allow energy to flow in either direction whether we are near the other person of not. The more energy that flows through the cord, the thicker it will be. Some connections are meant to be mutually beneficial, where we send love and light to each other regularly. But in moments of weakness, people often use cords to send feelings of anger or resentment outwards, or to gather energy from others without ever sending energy back to them, draining the other person of their energy. When you hear the term "psychic vampire", this is what people are referring to.

There is no reason for any of us to maintain cords of attachment. We have cords today because we have forgotten that we can be our own sources of energy and that we do not need to steal energy from outside of ourselves to light up our bodies. This is what we have been taught by mass consciousness, and something that we need to unlearn.

A good process to sever a cord is to see it dissolving into pure light. See the spot where the cord was attached closing, healing, and glowing as brightly and strongly as the rest of you. Repeat this with all the cords, one by one, or all at once, whichever works better for you. While you work, see if you gather any information on the people or beings the cords connected you to, and what the cords carried. When you have finished, ask Spirit to work with the light bodies of those people, to return them to their pure selves. Forgive yourself for any cords you may have placed on others, and forgive those that placed cords on you. Below, I've included a nice guided meditation you can read through here or listen to online at: www.mayacointreau.com/transform/light.mp3. Once you get the hang of identifying and dissolving cords of attachment, ask your guides to help you check yourself every month or so when you journey. Some guides excel at cord removal, gobbling them up like tasty treats, while other guides are great at helping you create better boundaries so you don't build new cords in the first place.

The Temple of the Light

To begin this meditation, take a deep breath, all the way into your solar plexus.

Breathe out.

Imagine that the air you breathe is made of pure light, and with each breath in, you illuminate your inner body. See the air radiate from your lungs outward, as the oxygen enters your bloodstream, lighting pathways to throughout your body. You are luminous, radiant, from within.

Breathe in, and breathe out.

With each breath go further into your own body, following the lit pathways. See the light growing brighter, until you are surrounded by nothing except pure radiance.

Continue to breathe slowly, deeply. Feel yourself becoming one with the light, becoming pure energy, floating gently. You have come to the Temple of the Light, where you will work with your light body and your gridwork.

Here, surrounded by Spirit, you will repair your light body and reintegrate it with your physical body.

When you are in your light body, you see with your mind's eye. As you look at yourself, surrounded by light, do you see any cords connected to your body?

When we exchange energy with other people, sometimes we form cords of attachment. These cords are designed to allow energy to flow in either direction whether we are near the other person of not. The more energy that flows through the cord, the thicker it will be. Some connections are meant to be mutually beneficial, where we send love and light to each other on a regular basis. But in moments of weakness, people often use cords to send feelings of anger or resentment outwards, or to gather energy from others without ever sending energy back to them.

There is no reason for any being to have cords of attachment. We have the cords today because we have forgotten that we can be our own sources of energy, and that we do not need to steal energy from outside of ourselves to light up our bodies. This is what we have been taught by mass consciousness, and something that we need to unlearn.

To begin, pick up one of the cords, and see the light that surrounds you infusing it. See it glowing, filled with energy, until it dissolves into pure light. See the spot where the cord was attached closing, healing, and glowing as brightly and strongly as the rest of you. Repeat this with all the cords, one by one, or all at once, whichever works better for you.

While you work, see if you gather any information on the people or beings the cords connected you to, and what the cords carried.

When you have finished, ask Spirit to work with the light bodies of those people, to return them to their pure selves.

Forgive yourself for any cords you may have placed on others, and forgive those that placed cords on you.

Now that you are whole again, examine your light body.

Do you see areas that look darker, or different from other areas? Look over your entire body on all sides, from your head to your toes. Remember to check all your limbs and organs, and take note of any areas that have lost their glow, look murky, or stand out in any other way.

Now visualize that your body is covered with a fine grid of blue light: the blue lines crisscross over you like neon lines from graphing paper. Make sure that your entire grid is intact and full of light. Repair any tears or problems you find, realigning your gridwork and filling it with blue light.

See the pure light of Spirit surrounding you, infusing the grid. The blue lines glow brilliantly, and your light body within radiates. See any areas that had been dim or discolored regain their vitality.

You are whole, you are strong, and you are energized. Take a moment to remember how this feels.

Look below you, and see your physical body. Feel your light body descend, buoyant and complete, slowly towards your physical body. Feel your light body enter the physical. Make sure that every limb, every muscle, every organ, is integrated, a matched pair.

Feel Spirit coursing along your veins, flowing in your blood, filling your entire body. As you breathe in, feel the energy and light ride into your lungs, carried with the air. Spirit is here for you always, the source of all.

Breathe in.

Breathe out.

When you are ready, return.

Lighting Your Inner Flame

We all falter under the daily grind of work, eat, sleep. Bad sleep habits, emotional strain, and the physical demands of hormonal changes and growing bodies take a major toll on energy levels, affecting our creativity and mood. It's hard work being a teen, and life only can get more complicated as you get older and have more responsibilities. In this chapter, we're going to look at some more ways you can work on balancing your health and energy levels so that you can have a more joyful experience here on earth.

In mythology, creative fiery energy is associated with the gods of the forge, Brigid, Vulcan, and Hephaestus; Vesta and the Kitchen God, gods of the hearth; and Pele, the Hawaiian volcano goddess. Also the sun, the lightning, the phoenix, dragons, and snakes – which brings us to **kundalini** energy. Kundalini is often referred to as the "fire serpent." It is described as a sleeping, dormant energy that in most people lies coiled at the base of the spine until it is awoken through conscious living. Once activated, kundalini runs up and down the spine or central pole, through all the chakras up to create a stronger bridge to the soul star chakra and allow us to receive more direct communication from Source and our higher selves. In some healing traditions, kundalini is also known as "body lightning" and it can feel like a tingle of electricity running up and down the body or a tremor in the tailbone or seat, as well as a cool or warm breeze across the palms and hands.

The caduceus, a familiar symbol used within the medical profession here in the West, is actually adapted from representations of kundalini and the rod of Asclepius, the Greek god of healing. The kundalini, the fire serpents, coil up the wand – our central nervous system and spine – and emerge as light above the crown, symbolizing the balanced hemispheres of the brain.

Kundalini activation happens easily and naturally with meditation, breathing practice, and focused physical exercise: it is one of the primary goals of traditional yoga studies. Kundalini activation tends to result in feelings of compassion, interconnectedness, and higher levels of focus and energy. Sounds nice, right?

Let's try a **Kundalini Activation Meditation**, you can listen along at: www.mayacointreau.com/transform/kundalini.mp3

Close your eyes and take a deep breath in. Breathe out. Breathe in. Breathe out.

Relax. Imagine you are surrounded by a huge glowing ball of light. The light is warm, pulsating. You feel safe and comfortable. Continue breathing deeply, in and out. With each breath in, see the ball contacting, getting smaller and more concentrated, as you draw the center of the ball into your body. See the ball centered in your root chakra, its boundaries getting close and closer to you, until it is finally a highly concentrated ball of energy residing deep within your body, in the base of your spine at your root.

Now see this ball of light, this ball of pure Qi, slowly uncoiling to take the form of a fiery serpent of light. You feel comfortable with the snake – it is your birthright, this snake, your body lightning, an old friend who has been with you, sleeping, all your life. Now see the snake begin to wind its way up your central pole, your spine, your central nervous system. It pauses at each chakra to awaken it with a flick of its tongue, as it travels slowly ever upwards. It awakens your first chakra. Your Tribal Center. Your Self-Confidence and Power. Your Heart Center. Your Center of Communication. Your Third Eye. Your Crown Chakra. Your ability to access communication directly from Source and Your Higher Self.

Your fire serpent stretches lazily now from your tailbone up around your spine to rest its head above your own. You feel energized and awakened, full of excitement like a child. Your kundalini has been activated. Take a moment now to engage with your kundalini, with your fire serpent, and with your higher self, your soul, and ask how you can keep this energy activated on a regular basis and if there is anything you can do to better incorporate the energy into your body and daily life.

Now thank your higher self, your physical body, and your kundalini.

Take a deep breath in, and a deep breath out. A deep breath in, and out.

Return.

Raising your kundalini isn't the only way to light that inner fire. The breath of fire from the first chapter is great, too. In fact, all forms are of physical exercise are good to increase and balance fire in the body. Here are two quick and easy things you can do:

HA! Airplane - to build your fire

Feet together, stand with your arms straight out sideways. Keeping your arms straight, swing your arms in front of you three times, crossing them, inhaling with each cross. After the third cross, swing your arms back out to your sides like a baby bird spreading its wings, rise up on your toes with your chest out and exhale a loud "Ha!" Repeat the sequence 5-10 times.

Woodchopper - to release excess fire energy.

Stand with your feet planted slightly wider than your hips. Raise your arms straight above your head with your hands clasped. Take a deep breath and arch back slightly, then exhale and swing your hands down between your legs, ending with a loud "Ha!" Repeat 3-10 times. Take your time, being careful not to become dizzy or strain your back with over-exuberance.

If you thought those were fun, you might enjoy **Qigong**. A Chinese system of energy manipulation over 2,500 years old, Qigong energizes and balances the physical body while strengthening the spirit. Qigong is related to martial arts as an exercise form. It also teaches balance and is believed to improve your ability to sense and treat dis-ease within your body. Remember the "Karate Kid" movie, when Mr. Miyagi partially healed Daniel's leg during the tournament? That was a perfect example of Qi Healing. As Mr. Miyagi says in the movie, his lessons with Daniel are "not just karate only. Lesson for whole life. Whole life have a balance. Everything be better. Understand?"

In all aspects of Qigong practice, there is a major focus on proper breathing. Make sure you breathe in through your nose – breathing through your mouth alone can easily decrease the amount of oxygen you take in by 15% or more. You can find some great Qigong videos on YouTube. Mimi Kuo-Deemer and David Beaudry are two of my favorites to watch. Check out their Eight Brocades, Five Element, Immortal Form, and Primal Qigong videos for some well-rounded routines that will balance all the elements of your body, mind, and soul. Similarly, **yoga** and **tai-chi** balance the elements through controlled movement and conscious breathing.

Still tired, even though you're sleeping, eating well, and moving around regularly? Your body might just be having a tough time dealing with the constant flux of stimuli coming from your nervous system and hormones. Instead of relying on energy drinks and snacks loaded with sugar and chemicals, try **herbs and teas** that can boost your brain and balance your hormones. Chaste Tree Berry has been used for centuries to regulate hormones, whether they are low or high, so that's a great one to research with your parents or guardians if you feel out of balance. Astragalus, Elderberry, Butterfly Pea Flower, Reishi, and Ginseng are all known to build Qi in the body and help us fight off germs — they're great to have on hand when the school year starts. Herbs in your kitchen like ginger, cinnamon, and cardamom are all warming and help the body wake up while moving toxins out — drinking chai is a good way to incorporate these herbs into your diet along with a mild caffeine boost.

Despite everything, sometimes you still might find yourself getting run down, sick, or injured. You can use the power of light to work with Spirit and help the body feel better. **The Iris Healing Method**™ is a form of light-energy healing that boosts healing on all levels by increasing the amount of light in our body. This method requires no specific training, it is an ancient human birthright. It comes to us through the light itself, through rainbows, space and time. Iris healing generates the full spectrum of light outside our normal sight range: it uses all light frequencies, every color ray, to heal all aspects of all levels of being. It works beyond all time, in all times, healing the past, the future, and above all, now. It is pure light, Source light, pure divine energy. It connects you to Spirit, to the God-spark in you, to all that is good and pure in you and the universe, physical and beyond.

Whenever you wish to use Iris Healing, simply envision a full spectrum light rainbow streaming in through your crown chakra and out through your hands as you direct the light out through your palms back into your own body or someone else's. If the person you want to help isn't with you, you can imagine you are cupping a miniature version of that person between your palms as you project a sphere of the rainbow light around them, or you can stream the rainbow light into a photo or symbolic image of that person. You can use Iris Healing when you're in class, when you're watching TV, when you're riding the bus. You can also use it outside of time and space, in your own healing sanctuary, a place you create through meditation that belongs to only you.

Sometimes, working on the body through a journey can be very effective, since all physical forms, including the human body, are created first as thoughtforms through an energetic matrix, sometimes known as the **etheric body**. It can be viewed as a light grid, and is often seen to be an electric blue construct of light. When you do energy work on the body, it is this grid that most often needs to be repaired. If you have ever seen 3D animation videos of works in progress, this idea can be easily visualized – the gridwork looks much like a wireframe of the physical object, but instead of existing under the skin, the gridwork overlays the body. Any disturbances in the etheric gridwork will result in imbalances in the physical body. Missing gridwork will result in damaged parts of the human body. You may or may not be able to see the etheric gridwork visually, but it can generally be sensed and repaired through meditation or journeywork. Let's create a special healing space for you now (listen to the meditation online at: www.mayacointreau.com/transform/heal.mp3)

Create Your Own Healing Sanctuary

To begin this meditation, take a deep breath.

Breathe in. Breathe out.

In, and Out.

Today, you will create a sacred space that exists for you, through you. With each breath go deeper within your body, until you reach your inner point of stillness, the quiet darkness where creation begins.

Here, anything is possible. You are a god within your own body.

Now, in your mind's eye, turn to the North, and see yourself in nature. This can be your favorite place, or somewhere you have never been before. Here it is just you, and the Earth.

Visualize every piece of grass, every stone. See them clearly, vibrant and real. Breathe life into them, so you can touch them, experience them fully. Feel yourself in this space.

Here you will build your own place for healing. It can be large or small, with many rooms, or none at all. On this journey, you will create every detail. This healing space will be a place you can return to again and again, for all time, to heal yourself and to heal others. It will belong to you. If you want, it can be a huge center for healing and learning complete with teachers and guides, or it can be a simple altar for healing in the woods, quiet and real. Here you can have seminars, learn any aspect of healing and evolution, and heal problems on the physical plane. You are the creator and the builder of your healing temple. You may call your guides to help you, or you can do it alone.

Relax, enjoy your time in your healing sanctuary, and return when ready. Know that you can return any time.

Living the Dream

Dreaming is so important to all of us. We all dream, whether we remember the dreams or not. Most animals have been shown to dream. Dreaming is where our soul takes flight. It's also another way we can connect with your true selves. Many cultures say the dreaming world is the real world, that our waking reality is the myth, the place we need to wake up from so that we can see the whole truth, the bigger picture — so we can connect with Source without the illusion of physical reality getting in the way. Of course, our souls chose to be born and we're here for a reason — we owe it to ourselves to explore this planet and all it has to offer as fully and joyfully as we can. When we can bring our soul and our physical existence into harmony, that's the real magic. Though it may seem counter-intuitive, **dreaming** can help with this.

There are many sorts of dreams, but I believe that they are all, in their own way, truly real. I believe that often while we dream our souls travel to other places and dimensions that exist both in and out of time. Sometimes we dream simply for fun or release, to work through problems that are bugging us during the day. Sometimes we dream so that we can change our future.

When I was pregnant with my second child my husband and I both had dreams about our daughter one night that were troubling. I had a very realistic birthing dream where she did not breathe: her skin was blue and she could not be resuscitated. The same night, my husband had a dream that he was walking with her toddler-self up some stairs at a baseball stadium, but then when he looked down she was no longer there. She was gone. I knew that these dreams were signs, and being only three or four months pregnant there was plenty of time to do something about them. I did several journeys for my daughter to be sure her lungs would form properly and any karmic issues were being released – when she was born she was huge, healthy and alert, and remains so to this day. She also has a strong, loud voice that projects much further than most peoples! If you are given a dream that feels prophetic you might be being given a chance to choose your future, to shift your reality. If events still progress the same way they did in the dream, that doesn't mean you failed, either — sometimes we are forewarned so that we can prepare mentally and emotionally, and know that we did everything we could. Our higher self doesn't want us to have regrets, and dreaming can help us live more freely.

It's not all fun and games though. Many shamans and lightworkers are assigned some of their most important work in the dreamtime. A great many lightworkers have enlisted to help the planet ascend to a higher state of being, that's why there are so many of us here now. In the dreamtime we often help in two ways – some lightworkers help perform "upgrades" to the physical body and its energy systems so that individual humans can integrate more of their soul purpose here on earth. Other lightworkers are working to raise the frequency of the entire planet and clear any energies that drag us down as a collective, which I'll talk about more later on.

Dreaming connects us to the higher realms, because it is the higher realms. In dreaming you can literally do anything or be anywhere. As you practice honing your dreaming skills, you will have clearer and more vivid dreams. You will be able to distinguish between the real and unreal more easily, both when you are sleeping and waking. You will also develop better skills for manifesting the life you want here on Earth.

There are three key steps to beginning your dream work:

The first step in becoming a better dreamer is to acquire a dream journal. You can use your meditation journal for this, but you'll need to keep it right next to your bed. Dream journals are invaluable for good dreaming practices.

Step two is to state your intent. At the start of the night, write down what you intend to dream about, and that you also intend to remember it. Your intent might be to ask for guidance, or to travel somewhere, or for a message. Tell yourself that you want to have clear dreams that you will remember when you wake. Repeat this intention a few times in your head or out loud as you fall asleep.

Step three happens when you wake up: immediately write down whatever you remember, even if it's just one word or a color. Don't make the mistake of thinking that because your dream is so clear you will remember it later after you shower.

You probably won't. Write it down right away, trying not to move around too much or turn on any lights, since both those things shift our brain waves quickly to waking states.

If you practice these three things each night and morning, you will reach a point where you can remember an entire dream in detail, and eventually even all your dreams from each night. It might take a few days, a few weeks, or even months, but eventually it will happen.

When you are recording your dreams, try to note how you felt emotionally and physically when you woke from the dream, as well as to make a title for your dream that captures the essence of its theme. These practices can help you later when you try to decipher its meaning, such as whether the dream was a way of working through your sub-conscious fears or if it was an actual warning. The more dreams you catalog, the more you'll start to notice themes in your dream landscapes and themes, so when a dream is really trying to get your attention you'll notice it because it will feel or look different from the others.

If you want to try to enhance your dreaming even more, do some meditations to open your third eye chakra, your personal portal to seeing your truth. A simple technique for opening the third eye uses the breath as you drift to sleep. I learned this technique from one of my own guides (Thor, if you can believe it!) and many of my students have reported great improvements after incorporating it into their nightly routines. I call it the **Third Eye Breathing Technique**.

As you may remember from the chapter about the chakras, your third eye rests in the center of the axis between your brow and zeal points. As you breathe in, imagine that you pull the air in through your nose, up through your brow portal back through the brain along its channel to your third eye center in the pineal gland. As you breathe out, push the air out through your throat, through your zeal point at the base of your skull to your third eye center in the pineal gland, out through your nose. The zeal point is also known as the "Well of Dreams" and helps open the door to the dreaming world. Continue this third eye breathing, creating a tidal pull to and from your pineal gland, to stimulate your third eye and your ability to dream clearly, for 10-20 breaths.

Breathwork like this also has the added bonus of balancing the sympathetic and parasympathetic nervous systems, creating a calm, relaxed state that harmonizes mind and body. Elongating your breath out relaxes the parasympathetic nervous system, which is helpful to reach brain states conducive to dreaming and trancework, and elongating the breath in relaxes the sympathetic nervous system and regulates involuntary functions like blood pressure, heart rate, circulation, and digestion.

Once you're having more dreams, some of them might catch your attention. You might find yourself wishing you could go back in to see how the dream ends, visit more with those fun people you met, or change something that happened that didn't feel good. Shamans perform **dream re-entry** all the time through journeying, and you can, too!

Think about the dream you want to re-visit and what you want to do there, and then drum yourself back into your dream. Once you are there you can spend as much time as you want consciously viewing any aspect of the dream scenes or changing the outcome of a dream that didn't seem positive, the same way I changed my daughter's birthing dream.

Lucid dreaming is another way to consciously work within a dream and is a primary goal of many dreamers. When you are lucid dreaming, you are conscious within the dreamtime. You can choose the actions you take, rather than just watching things unfold. You can control what appears and what disappears: you shape your dreamscape, shift reality. You can visit with other people, deliver a message, or have real heart-to-heart communication. You may have had some lucid dreaming moments already, times when you were dreaming and all of a sudden thought "hey, I'm dreaming!" and woke up or shifted the scene. Your goal as a shamanic lightworker is to be able to control the inception of these moments, so that you can lucid dream whenever you need to. We start, of course, with intent. Before you go to sleep, follow your dream practice of writing down and stating your intent. Write down in your dream journal "tonight I intend to be conscious and lucid while I am dreaming." As you lie down and drift off to sleep, say this to yourself several times. Do not be disappointed if it doesn't happen the first night. It might even take weeks or months.

Once you have a lucid dream, though, it will be easier to have more. The more you work with your dreams, whether it is through dream re-entry, recall, or lucid practices, the more confident you will feel in the waking world. You'll have a deeper understanding of your own psyche, and get clearer about your own hopes, fears, and boundaries.

Want to understand your dreams even better? A wonderful way to decode the language of your dreams is to **host a dream circle**. Get a few friends or family members together who like to dream, and meet every 4-6 weeks. Each person brings one dream with them to the circle, something they don't quite understand or maybe that bothered them a bit. Set out some snacks and refreshments so everyone feels comfortable — dream circles should be fun!

Once everyone is gathered and chatted for a bit, the first person tells their dream to the group. Then, everyone takes turns saying what the dream might mean to them if it were theirs. The most important thing to remember with dreams is that we each have our own dream vocabulary that filters our thoughts and experiences. Colors mean different things to different people – gray might signify sadness to you, or peace to your friend. Tornados might be exciting and energizing to your aunt, but they might terrify your best friend's little sister. So you always have to figure out your own meanings and decide which suggestions feel right and which don't. People can also point out the conventional literary meaning of a symbol, or the spiritual significance of an image to see if that helps the dreamer understand what the point of the dream might have been. Ideas which do not resonate with the dreamer are just as important as the ideas that do, because those differences help the dreamer crystallize what the dream does and does not mean. Always remember that only the dreamer can say for certain what their dream might mean.

You are the architect of your dreams, you and your soul. You build your reality, all of them, and through dreaming, you can build a clearer resonance with your soul that will allow you to harness all the beauty and wonder of Source. So you can bring it here. So you can build a better future.

Ad Astra

You have been born at the tail-end of a cycle of distortion for the paradigms of **masculine and feminine energy**. You're here now because it's time to heal these distortions and get empowered. To do that, you need to embody both aspects of Source in its most divine forms. The question is, how?

The masculine is the solar, supportive aspect of Spirit. It is the part that nurtures and fuels creation, the energy that drives will. It is best embodied by love and honor.

The feminine is the lunar, creative aspect of Spirit. Ever-changing, ever making. It the passionate seed of evolution, the will of Source to expand and manifest.

We know these aspects well in their distortions, where the feminine is receptive and meek, and the male is domineering, angry and controlling. The distortion is the root of much conflict both in personal relationships and the world, but we can repair it, starting with ourselves. To balance your masculine and feminine energies, we're going to work with the six-pointed star, or its three-dimensional manifestation, the **merkabah.**

A six-pointed star consists of two triangles, one pointing down (the feminine) and one pointing up (the masculine.) The old saying "As Above, So Below," is all about getting these triangles, these energies, to properly mirror and support one another. The masculine triangle draws down energy from Source, and grounds it in the physical. The feminine triangle draws energy up from the Earth and expands it into material being-ness. When you work with the star as a 3-D object, each triangle becomes a 4-sided pyramid, or tetrahedron. On their own, in sacred geometry tetrahedrons represent the energy of fire: indeed, the merkabah is an active, living matrix that can be used for creation. It is referenced in ancient Qabbalah texts as a fiery wheel, a vehicle allowing prophets and angels to travel the heavens. Every human has a merkabah that surrounds them on the astral plane — something we'll talk more about in a minute. This merkabah, when it is working properly, increases your energetic connection to the physical realm. Unfortunately, with the distortion of the masculine and feminine aspects of self which we discussed earlier, most people's merkabahs are not working as they should be. Indeed, for many people, they are not working at all.

So, how do we fix it? You make sure that it is fully powered up, shining and spinning.

When running properly, a merkabah is a vortex of manifestation, an energetic computational machine that interacts directly with Source to create the reality you are wanting. If you haven't consciously programmed it, it's not creating much of anything. Your merkabah is your creative matrix that allows you to combine your soul intention with the spark of god-energy and literally create your reality however you want. All that is required is for your merkabah to be actively spinning, which is done through breathing exercises and intention. Ideally, try to spend 3-5 minutes daily spinning your merkabah. The way this is done is to breathe deeply and visualize that you are rotating the feminine, down-pointing tetrahedron to your right or clockwise (creating a high-pressure vortex that draws energy upwards for creation) and rotate the masculine, up-pointing tetrahedron to your left or counter-clockwise (creating a low-pressure vortex that draws energy "down" from Source.)

With a couple months of practice, your merkabah should be reprogrammed and spinning regularly without maintenance. Your masculine and feminine aspects will come into balance on their own, you'll be able to focus more on what you want to create and you'll intuitively know what you need to do to support yourself. Besides helping energize your physical body and increase your connection to Source, this is useful, because your merkabah is an amazing tool for personal manifestation and creation. When it is spinning, all you have to do is instruct it as to what you would like it to create. If there is negative energy in a room emanating from a person or geopathic stress, you might program your merkabah to deflect it and shield you. If you are wanting a specific job, your merkabah can reach into the energy matrix of the Earth and help conspire to create this specific reality. Or, you can give overarching instructions such as "I program my merkabah to flow with ease in this physical earth reality and to see that all of my needs and desires are fulfilled for the highest good of all involved." You are the only one on earth who can work with or program your merkabah. No other human or healer may influence the programming of your merkabah, although a healer may work on your breathwork and energy patterning to help facilitate merkabah activation.

Another thing you can do to help heal the world is spin your merkabah and imagine yourself as a fractal, expanding that energy out into the world, realigning the masculine-feminine as it ever-expands. Fractals are, at their core, the repetition of one energy as it swirls ever-outward, repeating itself over and over in perfect resonance. In this way, you are, we are, all IS, perfect fractals of Source. We all hold that spark of divinity within and recreate it perfectly, exactly, in every wave and sine, in every atom, again and again.

Your merkabah can also be used to help you travel **the astral realm**. What's that? Well, the astral realm can best be described as another layer of this dimension. It is the energetic layer of the physical realm, the aspect of reality that blends thoughts, forms and souls without the finicky pretense of matter getting involved. Just as your body's energetic aspects can affect your physical health, what happens in the astral plane can bleed through into the physical. They overlap, one influencing the other. Most people get excited when they hear about the astral realm and ask "how can I go there?"

I've got some good news: you already astral travel all the time! All humans have out-of-body experiences (or OBEs) while they sleep and dream, visiting other places and times, though not everyone remembers. Most astral work occurs while our body is in its deepest sleep state, and can be quite difficult to recall since the conscious, physical mind of the body remains completely uninvolved during this time. In fact, some people's very early childhood memories indicate that infants spend most of their time out of their bodies, observing their surroundings both with the eyes of their bodies and from across the room or above the heads of everyone else. As we grow up and become more accustomed to the earthly plane, we become more and more attached to our bodies, spending fewer waking moments in astral form.

In addition to the freeform exploration through the astral planes that we sometimes remember as dreams, we all have astral "jobs" that we do night after night. You might teach people to fly, help rewire people's brains to function better, clean up stale earth energy, or ferry souls into the light. When you drum and journey, you astral travel, too. Wouldn't it be cool, though, if you could do it when you were conscious and awake? Well, you can!

The easiest way to do that is to work with some sort of astral vehicle, an astral container for our consciousness. Astral travel happens most easily when one is in a completely relaxed state. Many people do well experimenting with astral travel just before they go to sleep, or after deep meditation. Playing music that is designed to help you produce more delta brain waves is very helpful. Still, you might find yourself yearning for more conscious control of your astral trips. If so, an astral vehicle like the merkabah might be just what you are looking for.

Astral vehicles allow us to do everything a skilled traveler can do – transcend time and space to be somewhere in an instant, fly through walls, and, perhaps best of all, it tends to lend a feeling of security to our consciousness. Many people have a hard time astral traveling at will because of fear or other inhibitions – using an astral vehicle can help us overcome these obstacles. Your astral vehicle can be anything you want: Wonder Woman's invisible plane, a body of light or light body, a bird, a spaceship, a sphere, a merkabah. Anything. Many people believe that shamans using animals as astral vehicles is the basis for shapeshifting folklore. The key is to find out what is going to work best for you. You want a vehicle that will give you the utmost control and peace of mind while you are traveling.

Once you know what your vehicle will be, relax and imagine a peaceful glow radiating throughout your body, relaxing your limb by limb, cell by cell. Take as much time as you need for this. Tension dissolves. Negative emotions are replaced by peace and love. You feel at ease and at peace.

Next, imagine your astral vehicle beginning to take form a few feet away from you. Pull Source energy in through your crown chakra and visualize it flowing out through you in a steady brilliant stream, charging your vehicle with energy and form. Imagine every detail of your vehicle as you work. See the size, the feel, the color, the quality of your vehicle.

Once it is fully charged, your astral creation must be given purpose and duty. Will your intention in clear, defined language to the vehicle. Tell your creation that it is an astral mode of transport for safe and limitless exploration and that when you have finished it shall return you to your physical body in this dimension.

Once your vehicle has been programmed, it is ready for you to enter. This is done by transferring your consciousness into the vehicle and is considered one of the most reliable methods for learning to astral travel. It can take a few tries, but essentially all you are doing is shifting your consciousness from one vehicle to another, like getting in a cab. Imagine yourself in the vehicle you so thoughtfully designed and program. Look around from within the vehicle, with your astral view. Take some time feeling comfortable in your construct.

If you like, you can just spend time looking around, getting used to the feel, or you can will your vehicle to go wherever you like – a simple thought will get you there. Your consciousness is the motor, the driver, and the road all in one.

If you find yourself suddenly back in your body, don't worry, just get right back in the vehicle again – it will be waiting for you nearby. Once you've done that, all you need to do is spend some time visualizing it next to you while you relax or meditate, really feeling it there in all its astral glory, and then shift your consciousness into the vehicle for takeoff.

Most people don't actually go anywhere right away – in fact, simply sitting in your vehicle, next to yourself, gazing around the room from this new perspective, is a great way to spend your first time. Astral views tend to be 3D, since we aren't constrained to forward seeing eyes, so this can take some getting used to.

As always, know that your consciousness can not get lost or trapped anywhere else. You will always return to your body the moment you will it, or if your body "needs" you (for a trip to the bathroom, to scratch an itch, etc.) Fear is not a mind-killer, but it IS an astral buzzkill!

When it's time to return, you might find yourself instantly back in your body at will, or you might decide to fly back in your vehicle and transfer consciousness back to your body. This is where your consciousness naturally wants to be, so it is easy and almost instantaneous. When you return, feel yourself fully in your body. Clench your hands. Wiggle your feet. Perfect. Finish up by imagining your beautiful vehicle dissolving into light, and call the light into your body, reabsorbing the pure Source energy and all the memories of your journey. You always want to make sure that you take the time to dismantle your creation. Otherwise, it could take several days to dissolve on its own – while it bumps around and follows you the whole time. Since it is essentially created by your own auric energies, these creations tend to stay with us. This could make you feel haunted or crowded at worst. At best, it's astral pollution, and no one likes a litterbug, whatever dimension we're in.

Speaking of creations that like to stay with us, another thing I should mention is the double. There are many words for this, in many traditions, including the fetch, or the doppelganger but the most common seems to center on the concept of "double." Why, and what is it? The double is an astral projection that is identical to us. You may see it when you are near your body, and most people believe it is another astral vehicle that is available for our use – a way of being in two places at one time, even. Others believe it is our mental body, or our etheric/energetic body, the thoughtform that creates our physical body which is visible to us from the astral plane. That explanation does present good logic for why it is generally encountered only if we are near our physical body, though it can wander. Perhaps you can find out the truth on your own astral journeys.

Astral pollution is just one form of energetic pollution that affects our physical reality. Many dreamers and shamans report working in the astral realms to clear the earth's atmosphere of old stagnant energy, which surrounds the earth both in our lower atmospheres and reaches far into the solar system away from our planet. Robert Monroe described it as actual soul pieces that are stuck in their own illusions of reality – souls who have left their physical bodies, died, but not moved back into the light or reincarnated. Some are down here as ghosts, wandering, while some are little further out. Some souls think they are already in heaven, inhabiting astral fantasies, refusing to move on. Some are lost pieces of souls that were scared away in traumatic events, hiding out until they feel safe to return to their larger soul. The thing they all have in common is that none of them are reconnecting with the fullness of their own full soul; they aren't connecting with their soul groups between lives to regroup, learn and plan, they aren't reincarnating; and they aren't connecting with Source. The other thing they have in common is that they are ALL, every one of them, creating shroud around the earth that makes the atmosphere heavier and heavier, making it harder for other souls to move through it and move on, and making it hard for good energy to get through to us. So, as I said, a lot of lightworkers are working each night to remedy this situation. These people are truly letting in the light! They spend a lot of time with each soul, one-on-one, helping it get out of its own way, gently convincing it to move past the illusions it has created (because whether they are beautiful or scary, the false realities these souls create are all illusions that hold back the soul), and move on to the next level of being. This, in turn, is allowing the earth to lift its vibration, and even helps our physical atmosphere improve.

One group of souls (both incarnated and non-incarnated) who work on this are called the blue triangle people, or the purple triangle people, because if you happen to get a photo of them it will look like a blue or purple triangle or merkabahs, and you can call on them to clear spaces of entities and lost souls who need to move on. Anytime you feel like there is a being or energy around you that you feel doesn't belong, lift your arms and raise your voice and call on them, asking them to take whatever is there back to the light, generally within 1-3 days, though very stubborn "ghosts" might need a few weeks of counseling to be convinced it's time to move on, back to stardust and light.

The Circle of Life

When we are angry or sad, those emotions become stored in our energy fields, messing with our whole system. Luckily we live within a physical plane that incorporates the concept of "Time" and so we have a buffer of time between our thoughts and when they manifest — we have time to remedy negative thought imprints before they manifest in our bodies or our lives. Take steps to love yourself and the life you lead, and you will begin to improve your reality in ways you may not even have dreamed of.

We've talked about how fun and helpful exploring other realities can be through meditation, dreamwork, and journeying, but there's still one more astral realm we haven't touched upon which we can access for self-healing.

A realm that exists outside of physical reality and the constraints of time, where our concept of time is considered an illusion. A realm of pure Source that contains the records and blueprints not only of your past and current lives, but also of your "future" or parallel lives. The memory of all living things, the history of all of Source, all of creation: the **Akash** is the etheric blueprint of all that has been or will ever be.

Each of us is part of the Akash. Each of us has our own Akashic "record", or pieces of the Akash that pertain to us specifically. When you know how, you can access the Akash to clear old trauma or baggage; shift your own energy; and program changes into your etheric blueprint, the energetic gridwork or roadmap for your physical body. Working with the Akash can show us what is really going on in a situation behind the scenes – such as when a relationship is compounded by old issues from other lifetimes.

When you heal something in the Akash, it shifts your energetic blueprint which creates a ripple effect in the physical world. Your health can shift, your life experience can shift. You can heal things that have been passed down from generation to generation within your family or your soul group, working with your DNA karmically. There are old belief-systems related to the idea of **karma** that say that the bad things you did in the past must be atoned for and that you will be rewarded for your good deeds — that what you do comes back to you. While positive actions can have positive results, the notion that Source seeks to punish us with our own karma is false.

In reality, it is our old emotional attachments to these misdeeds or heroic acts that affect us throughout our lives, our guilt and our anger, our ability to look at life joyfully and feel comfortable with ourselves.

That is what karma's really about at the soul level. That is how our old emotional baggage can become a program we act out again and again, like a song playing on repeat. When you take action to investigate the old belief system that is behind such programs, you can consciously release the need to engage in that drama and design a new soundtrack for your life.

There are lots of ways to enter the Akash and examine the past so you can let go of the old karma - remember, karma doesn't follow anyone: *we* hold onto *it*.

You can journey or meditate with your guides to look at your Akash and ask for help to release different patterns you see playing out in your life. Generally what your guides will show you is that there is a root cause for this pattern, a self-limiting belief that began years, or even lifetimes, ago. Beliefs like: "I'm not worthy of love," "Bad things always happen when I stand up for myself," and "Money is the root of all evil" are just a few examples of the kinds of inner beliefs that can limit our own happiness and success. If you don't feel like journeying on the pattern, you can find your buttons and triggers with one of the methods from the chapter on "What's Your Damage" and then use the same techniques to release the self-limiting beliefs that were described there. EFT, positive affirmations, statements of intention, toning, and healing meditations are all good methods for shifting your internal belief systems and energetic hang-ups.

Vow Breaking and **Fire Ceremonies** are powerful methods that can be used alone or be combined to great effect. Throughout our other lives, we have taken many vows, made many contracts, often without any sort of time limit on them. Since there is no such thing as time, these vows can carry over from year to year, life to life. Vows of poverty, vows of chastity, vows of obedience, devotion, love, silence, self-sacrifice, suffering, retribution, humility, and so on. We may have vowed never, ever to do something again, or we may have vowed to never stop trying to do something else. In the heat of the moment, we might have made a pact to never forgive someone or an oath to never bother speaking the truth again after being punished for a crime we did not commit.

These vows we've made, they still matter. A part of us still remembers them and may feel obligated to stick to them even though they hold no bearing or benefit for our current life. These vows manifest their effects on our lives much like karma, except they affect our judgment, our desires, and predilections. Some vows even have to do with old agreements that may have bound you to other people through cords of attachment. Rather than live beholden to old vows and a subconscious fear or reluctance to break them, free yourself by releasing these vows.

To **release your vows**, create a sacred space and relax.

Call in your guides and higher self.

Now state loudly and clearly with intention:

"I am one with my spark-of-god-self, my higher, greater self, with all of my soul, and the light of Source. With conscious intention, we completely release and sever each vow, contract, oath, pact, program, and agreement we have made or ever will make with ourselves or with others that does not serve our highest good. The lessons I have learned through these vows remain, but the obligations are now ended. All vows, pacts, oaths, programs, and contracts made against me are also now revoked and the connections are severed. This is my will, make it so."

You can thank your guides now and release the space, or you might want to journey to your sacred healing place for further cleansing and clarity, or do some transfigurational toning to break apart the vows. With a grownup's permission, you can also work with the element of fire to break and release old contracts using one or more candles. Fire is one of the most powerful, simple and accessible tools we have for transformation. Fire elementals hold amazing co-creative power. The simple act of calling them in as we write down what we wish to transmute or release, and then burning it, should not be underestimated. This act can be done with a candle, intending that as the candle burns down, the result manifests. Or it can be done with a larger fire, where wood is placed with intention and layered with smudge, and the flames are called with intention, and the objects/written intentions burned are released.

A **fire ceremony** can be as simple or as complex as you wish. Writing out and then drawing your intention of a vow release and how you will grow from the end of the contract can be extremely cathartic. Speaking your intentions loudly and with feeling empowers your ritual – but you can also whisper it, or growl it. Many traditions actually encourage the development of a "ritual voice" which uses low guttural speech or a husky whisper. Fire ceremonies can also be used to bring your desires to life, manifesting or releasing whatever you intend.

They can be long and involved, or short and simple. Choose what you would like to invoke in your life, and write or choose a prayer or words that call in that energy. Inscribe a candle with your prayers or words. Create a sacred space to burn your candle, somewhere you can sit nearby while it burns safely in a bowl or glass container. Call in Spirit and your guides, and ask for their assistance in your prayers. State your intention, and light your candle. As it burns, your prayers will be sent to Spirit. Drum your prayers to Spirit for as long as you like. When the candle has burned down, dispose of its remains in a sacred place, such as buried at the base of a tree or plant or in your own fireplace (returning fire to fire).

Remember: *Always get an adult's permission to use candles and fire; they'll be able to help you set things up safely. Always have water, sand, or a working fire extinguisher on hand when you are working with fire energy!*

Want to dive further into your history and examine how other lifetimes may be impacting your present situation or mindset? Here's a meditation with one of the best fire guides, Dragon, that you can use to easily access any life you wish — or at least, the ones your higher self is ready to work on at the moment. (www.mayacointreau.com/transform/lives.mp3)

The Temple of Lives

To begin this meditation, you take three deep breaths. One for the past, one for the Present, and one for the Future.

Breathe in. Breathe out.

Breathe in. Breathe out.

Breathe in. Breathe out.

With each breath go deeper within your body, and feel yourself return to the Seat of the Four Elements, high on the Mountaintop. Darkness is falling, and the stars are coming out, twinkling around you.

Breathe in. Breathe out.

Far away in the sky, you see a glimmering point of light, shimmering and twinkling more than the other stars. The light grows bigger, brighter, like a comet streaking through the night sky.

You watch as it grows closer, and begin to discern a tail, undulating behind it, no ordinary comet. Closer and closer, until you realize you are seeing a dragon, smiling and streaking lazily towards you. You feel no fear, only curiosity. What is a dragon doing here, now?

The dragon continues approaching, very large now, the length of one, maybe two buses, and pulls up to the mountain peak, hovering a few inches off the ground in front of you.

"Hop on," it says. Its scales gleam in the darkness, and patches of soft fur along its back warm you as you nestle in and hold on.

The dragon rises up, and takes off, flying back out into the night, higher and higher, into the silent space of the sky, and beyond.

You fly through the atmosphere, past the moon, past the planets. Mars goes by, red, and Jupiter, larger than you ever imagined, and on, and on.

You fly past Saturn, and its rocky rings, past all the planets, and find yourself in the darkest part of our solar system, far among its boundaries, the dragon has landed on a very small round object, a planet, asteroid or moon, you aren't sure which. It is made of a dark, rough rock, and in the low light you can barely make out a small structure twenty feet away.

"That," says the dragon, "is the Temple of Lives. Enter, and I will wait here to carry you home."

You walk to the temple, closer, and now you can see that it is made of a pure white material, translucent. The temple is simple, just four standing stones, and four stone caps connecting them. It reminds you of Stonehenge, except that this was built by no man.

Light seems to come from the stones themselves, and as you look around you, the stones seem to come to life, images flitting across the stones, around you, above you, and a quiet whispering of voices from the stones surrounds you.

You have come to the Temple of Lives. Here you can review all lives, present, past and future, yours and others. The temple is here to help you in your spiritual evolution, to understand how you have chosen, and where you are heading.

As you choose a life to watch, its images will grow larger, surround you, its sounds will grow louder and others will fade away. When you've seen enough and you're ready to return, fly back with your dragon through the sky, back into your world.

Everyone's on the Spectrum

We're all always trying to make sense of the world, to see where things fit and where things don't. People love to put other people into boxes, the same way little kids like to line up toy cars in order of size or color. The world has all kinds of labels for different ways of being human. They try to classify us into races, sexes, nationalities, classes, and creeds. But we are all just people. In the end, we are all born, we all breathe, our hearts beat, we laugh, we love, we cry, and we die. In the spiritual community, you might hear all sorts of names for different types of people, too. **Indigos. Crystallines. Millennials. Rainbows.** People might tell you your aura is a special color and try to tell you that you are a certain kind of person — not realizing that auras are all colors at all times, shifting and evolving over each day throughout our entire lives.

Older generations are always trying to single out the differences between them and younger generations, so they can "fix" them. Younger generations are tasked with the job of stimulating previous generations so that humanity can continuing its evolutionary march. Recent generations have been given many names, most of them having to do with some colors in the aura that one or two people saw in a handful of kids decades ago. So, let's not worry too much about the labels, and let's talk instead about some of the things that make humanity's newest generations different.

You don't respect authority for authority's sake. People need to earn your respect and prove that what they are trying to teach you is worthy of your attention. Teachers call lots of you ADD or ADHD, claiming you can't pay attention, but it's really the opposite. Your brain is hardwired to notice everything and discern patterns more effectively, so the harsh lights and rigid decor at school can be overstimulating. You see the bigger picture, so you can tell what details are really worth paying attention to. If the information is sub-standard, you're not going to want to assimilate it. This means that teachers are having to re-evaluate decades of standards in teaching, create new curriculums and work harder. Go easy on them. Even the worst teachers started out with one thing in their hearts: a desire to help children learn and grow. You can make it more difficult for them, or you can try and help them help you by reminding them in little ways of why they became teachers in the first place. A smile and friendly hello each day are a good way to start.

You have more empathy for all of humanity and you worry about the state of the world. You feel better when you can move around and be free, especially when it's outside. Grounding and eating right will really help you stay in balance here, so try to take care how you treat your body. Volunteer work is a great way to empower your soul and relieve some of your worries about different issues like pollution, racism, homelessness, or animal welfare.

You're project-oriented, happier when you have a tangible goal you can work toward. You learn differently than other people, but you also see things differently, too, meaning that you can see solutions where maybe other people can't. Talk to your parents or a teacher to see if there's something you care about that you can work on for extra credit. Maybe you can create a new club, maybe you just need to step outside the box and follow your heart. Sometimes, the world just needs one strong teen to lead the call to action — don't believe me? Look up Greta Thunberg, Yash Gupta, Malala Yousafzai, Easton LaChappelle, Autumn Peltier, Louis Braille, Ryan Hreljac, and Julia Bluhm.

"Grown men may learn from very little children, for the hearts of little children are pure, and, therefore, the Great Spirit may show to them many things which older people miss." ~Black Elk, Medicine Man of the Oglala Lakota

Black Elk had many visions of the environmental and humanitarian issues his own people and the world would suffer. He also foretold that future generations would return to the old ways, respecting the earth and working with Great Spirit, and heal the world. As a young person, it's your right to remind the rest of the world what matters, what we need to do next. To see the things we're missing, to let us know how you want us to shape your world, how we can help you reach your brightest future. The adults around you will do the best they can, but every generation has its own concerns, its own paradigms it has to smash, so our concerns might not be yours — and your own children will someday show you new things, too. It's up to you now to reach for the stars and light your own way.

Interestingly, scientists now say that we all come from the stars, that each atom in our body emerged from an exploding star eons ago. Many tribes around the world believe that we, people, also came from the stars. Some legends talk about sky people, such as the thunderbeings of legend. Some legends talk about gods visiting from above and mixing their blood or mating with humans, to create the people we are today. Still others say that the first people on earth climbed down ladders through holes in the sky and then created the land itself from the depth of the oceans. Were these holes in the sky actually wormholes or spaceships? Was earth terraformed? We'll probably never know the whole story, no matter how much science and religion keep looking, but one thing is certain. You are stardust. The matter in your body came from the light, a burst of starlight in an infinite void, just like your spirit.

Lots of people now believe that we incarnate also in the parallel dimensions and worlds, in multiple timelines and bodies. The lives your soul has experienced comprise your spiritual lineage. Some cultures believe that you carry bits of DNA with you from lifetime to lifetime, with your soul -- a sort of karmic DNA. If this is true, it means the legends are true, and some of your stardust may also carry DNA from other worlds. These off-world karmic and genetic lineages are often referred to as your **Starseed** lineage or family.

There are many, many starseed families. Some that you might be familiar with from TV or other books are: Arcturian, Pleiadian, Whispers, Elven, Fairy, Sirians, Orion, Spider, Lyran (cat), Reptilian, Blues, Greys, Draconian. There are many more, and subsets of each. Some families overlap or descend from another, just like here on earth. Some have troubled pasts and fight amongst themselves, not unlike humanity.

We are all just aspects of each other.

Whether you believe in aliens or not, I find connecting starseed families can be helpful because it helps us see what archetypal issues we might be working on here in this lifetime: power struggles; material survival relating to things like money or having a safe place to live; giving and receiving love; helping others; or using or own inner magic and power for good. Doing journeywork to connect with your starseed aspects can be really fun and beautiful, taking you to gorgeous new worlds. Then when you return, you can think about the best parts of those places and figure out how to manifest more of that life, here. Likewise, your starseed families can act as guides for this lifetime to help you solve problems they might have suffered from. When you work with guides like starseeds, you're really just tapping into the vast pool of mass consciousness for insight and wisdom you might not be able to access on your own: the wisdom of the collective, an imaginative think-tank powered by the stars reaching for a more positive reality.

Walking the Path

Moving forward, what do you want your life to look like?

Everyone walks a different path. Where will yours lead?

Will it be a path with a heart? Will it speak to your soul? Native Americans say we should all travel the Good Red Road and I think they have the right idea. The Good Red Road takes you from youth and passion to wisdom and a return to Spirit here on Earth. When you walk the Good Red Road, you are in balance and harmonized with the world around you. You are considerate and compassionate. You are generous and acting for the highest good, including your own. You leave a smaller footprint, you give thanks to the plants and the animals, and you try to make the world a better place.

"One may be of any race or of almost any religion and walk the Red Road. The Road is a path, away. Its full meaning is the way one acts, the methods one uses, and what directs one's doing. There is more to the Red Road then spoken word or written words on paper. It is behavior, attitude, a way of living, a way of "doing" with reverence – of walking strong yet softly, so as not to harm or disturb other life." — John Redtail Freesoul

As a being of immense light and power, remember to stay in the glow of Source. When you feel lost, look to Spirit. When you are rushed and overwhelmed, slow down. Breathe deeper, meditate more. When you are distraught and hurting, reach out to your guides – they will do all they can to raise your vibration and shift you towards healing in the easiest manner possible. When you have a choice to make, ask yourself, does this path have a heart? Does it make me feel lighter or heavier? More joyful or less happy?

Always, follow the joy, follow the path with a heart. Make decisions that make your heart expand, that make your soul sing. Be thankful and express gratitude for the little things that you do have, and don't allow worry to cloud your thoughts — don't borrow trouble from a future that may never come. Take each day moment by moment. When a thought pops into your head, "Wouldn't it be nice if I..." grab hold of that thought. Feed it. Keep it growing, keep it going. Respect the process, expect the better outcomes, and know that there is no order of miracles according to Source, no act too big or too small to conceive, no goal too large or too hard to achieve. In the eyes of Source, all outcomes are equal, the only difference is whether they developed in an environment of fear or joyful expectation. Pay attention to what makes you feel better, and what makes you feel worse. Do more of what makes you feel better.

Just be you. Be the person you intended to become when you were born. No one enters this life thinking, I'm going to be in this body, and I'm going to limit my options, and starve my body, and feed my mind fear. No, of course not. Before you were born you thought to yourself, "Now here is this great little body that has so many possibilities, and though there will be some challenges it is going to be so very interesting to find ways to create the best possible outcomes and enjoy the unlimited potential of this world. I can't wait to get started!"

That is what you thought, and don't you owe it to yourself to begin living the way you intended? Give yourself up to the wonder of the unfolding that is the perfect you. Start today. Make room in your life for good things to happen by releasing some of your baggage. Pay attention to synchronicities and coincidences, each of those little love letters from the universe letting you know that Source notices you, Source cares.

Don't be afraid to take time for yourself, to nurture yourself. The world needs you to be whole. The world needs you to be well. The world needs you to be filled with light and love, shining that blessed radiance that is uniquely YOU all over the place.

Lifting other people up.

Healing the world.

Being you.

Find What You Need

There are many exercises in this book and you might not be sure which ones to use sometimes. If there is even just one practice in all of these pages that you enjoy doing week-to-week, that will be enough to help shift your mindset significantly and trigger improvements in your life.

This index contains a **master list of exercises** in order of appearance and what they are good for, as well as an alphabetical **table of situations and tools** that can help in the moment. There are more than seventy powerful exercises and tools for transformation here, include ten meditations with downloadable audio files.

Remember, life is a process! The more you can let go of the end result and simply enjoy each step along the way, the better life will become.

The Master List

Four-Fold Breath is a calming practice that deepens the breath, encourages physical awareness, and stimulates cellular healing in the body. (5)

Breath of the Sun boosts the immune system and increases physical energy. (7)

Breath of the Moon calms the nervous system and relaxes the body. (7)

Breath of Fire stimulates digestion, boosts the metabolism and warms the body. (7)

Finger Massage balances the five elements through massaging each finger on both hands (or toes on the feet) by stimulating the meridians. Thumb for ether, index for air, middle for fire, ring for water, and pinky for earth. (157)

Bhudi Mudra balances your ether and earth elements, helping you connect your body and spirit. It is often used to enhance communication, intuition and psychic abilities. (9)

Ahamkara Mudra is used to combat fear and is believed to raise self-confidence. (9)

The Kubera mudra is called the "Make a Wish" mudra. Use this mudra with any deep breathing exercise to center and align yourself to your soul purpose and desire. (9)

The Mukula mudra is used most often to instigate healing in the body. All five elements are brought together to create harmony. (9)

Brain Wave Music uses special frequencies, tones and beats to synchronize the left and right hemispheres of the brain, raise or lower your dominant brain wave state so that you can sleep more deeply, study more effectively, or access creativity. (15)

Drumming, Singing Bowls and Rattles easily shift the brain to slower brain wave cycles that encourage meditation, relaxation, creativity, focus, and clarity. A drumming track recorded by the author for journeying can be accessed online at **mayacointreau.com/transform/drumming.mp3** (16)

Chanting is the vocal repetition of syllables or phrases. The action of chanting relaxes the mind, balances hormones and the immune system, and connects your intentions with Source energy. (17)

Toning & Groaning allows your voice to express itself without a filter, smashing through blocked energy in the body, releasing pent up emotions, and allowing the body to relax. (17)

If it were me... is a phrase that can be employed to enhance compassion and put yourself in other people's shoes. (24)

It's all part of you helps you look at people and situations non-dualistically. Whatever you admire, you also hold inside of you; and the things that irritate or sadden you also mirror aspects of yourself that can actually make you a stronger, better person. (37)

Trace the Trigger allows you to follow line of reasoning back to the true source of your frustration and emotional distress to the parts of you that need the deepest healing. (39)

Emotional Freedom Technique combines positive statements with tapping movements on the body to allow deep emotional releases and helps the body and mind work together as a team. (40)

Freewriting loosens up rigid thinking and encourages you to open up, both creatively and emotionally. (44)

Automatic Writing is a type of freewriting that encourages you to have a dialogue with your inner emotions, you higher self or soul, and your spiritual guides. (47)

Bullet Journaling tracks goals and habits through the week, month, and year so that you can see what you've achieved, how you are evolving, and figure out what is really important to you in the moment. It can be combined with freewriting and art booking practices to encourage creativity. (49)

Loving Kindness Meditation fosters compassion and goodwill for all beings, including yourself, loved ones, and even perceived enemies. (62)

Positive Affirmations retrain the belief systems of mind, body, and soul through the repetition of positive statements. (65)

Give Yourself a Hug uses the physical benefits of self-embrace to release endorphins in the body and calm the nervous system. (66)

Ho'oponopono is a modern Hawaiian practice of forgiveness and compassion that fosters community healing and helps release grief, anger, and fear. (69)

Blessing Boxes help you focus your intentions and use the power of daily affirmations or prayer to create positive outlooks and change. (74)

Vision Boards can be used to help keep you on track in a project, clarify your dreams and desires, and create more positive emotions about your current situation. (75)

Transfigurational Toning can be used for healing, to energize a space, or to empower ones intentions. (75)

The I AM accesses the highest aspects of yourself to be the best you can be. (79)

The Temple of Inspiration connects you to your higher self for wisdom, creativity, and inspiration. Access the meditation here: mayacointreau.com/transform/inspiration.mp3 (81)

The ABCs activate, align, balance, clear, connect, and stabilize your chakras and aura. (94)

Negative Ion Exposure encourages feelings of well-being and ease, improve mood and help the body naturally fight off oxidative stress. Visit mountains, waterfalls, and oceans for maximum exposure. (97)

Earthing allows you to discharge free radicals and soak up negative ions by walking barefoot. (97)

Imagine You Are a Tree to ground your energy, release and cleanse excess of distorted energy, or to connect with the planetary grid of mass consciousness. (98)

Tighten Your Silver Cord to strengthen your will to live and have a more grounded, comfortable existence here on planet Earth. (106)

Postive Boundaries are important. They help us respect ourselves and our bodies, and the emotions and bodies of other people. Remember, "No" is a complete sentence. (108)

The Pyramid of Protection can be used to add an extra layer of protection to your auric field through simple visualization, or a more in depth meditation can be accessed here: <u>mayacointreau.com/transform/protection.mp3</u> (111)

Mountain Grounding creates a deeply protected feeling in the body. You cannot be moved. You cannot be swayed. You have the power of the mountain behind you. (115)

The Temple of the Open Heart is a great place to visit to work through any issues relating to grief, trauma, abuse, relationship issues, or boundary problems. Experience the meditation at <u>mayacointreau.com/transform/openheart.mp3</u> (120)

Eating & Sleeping Well create a strong foundation for physical, mental and emotional health. (124)

Essential Oils shift our mood by enhancing our brain chemistry, have anti-inflammatory and healing effects, and cleanse bacteria, viruses, and molds from the air, surfaces and our bodies. (129)

Sway Testing is a bio-feedback technique that allows you to connect with your body and higher self and get information right from the source that is critical to your own self-healing. (131)

Body Mapping gives you an intuitive snapshot of what's going on in your body and energy field. (134)

Light Therapy uses different wavelengths of light to stimulate cellular healing, decrease inflammation, and detoxify the body. (140)

Chromotherapy uses the power of color to encourage cellular healing and improve mood or energy levels. (141)

Hydrochromopathy energizes water with color for chromotherapeutic uses. (143)

Art Booking is a great tool for allowing your creativity to shine and give yourself a safe space for self-expression. (148)

The Medicine Wheel reminds you to stay centered and balanced through attention to all the elements. (157)

The Seat of the Four Elements is a meditation that will help you connect more strongly with each of the elements. (mayacointreau.com/transform/fourelements.mp3) (159)

Crystals and Stones give you something tangible to hold onto in your pocket and are like little friends that are constantly working to ground, protect, and encourage you. (165)

Connecting with Your Guides allows you to access a non-physical team of cheerleaders and teachers who will help you on your journey through life. (173)

The Temple of Guidance is a meditation with at will help you connect to a new personal guide and get the answers you need. (mayacointreau.com/transform/guidance.mp3) (178)

Shamanic Journeying is a more active form of meditation that allows the soul to travel to other worlds and dimensions, perform self-healing, and connect with guides. Listen to this audio file to be guided through your first journey: mayacointreau.com/transform/firstjourney.mp3 (182)

Cord Removal helps you maintain positive boundaries and make sure that no one in draining your energy (or vice versa). Remove them on your own or visit **The Temple of the Light** for help with the process using this online meditation: mayacointreau.com/transform/light.mp3 (185)

Kundalini Activation allows your body to run higher levels of source energy through the chakras. Do the meditation here: mayacointreau.com/transform/kundalini.mp3 (191)

HA! Airplane activates the fire and air elements in the body and energizes body and mind. (194)

The Woodchopper allows you to release excess fire energy. (194)

Qigong is an ancient Eastern practice that balances the elements in the body and allows you to harness and direct Qi, or universal life energy. **Yoga** is also a balancing practice for the elements in the body. (195)

Herbs and Teas have many uses, including relaxing the mind, soothing inflammation and stress, detoxing the body, and balancing hormones. (196)

The Iris Healing Method™ accesses and channels the full spectrum of light to stimulate cellular healing. (196)

Create a Healing Sanctuary where you can work on healing physical ailments for yourself and loved ones through meditation. (mayacointreau.com/transform/heal.mp3) (198)

Third Eye Breathing calms the nervous system and activates the pineal gland so that you can access deep sleep for dreamwork with ease. (203)

Dream Journaling helps you discern dreaming patterns, develop a deeper relationship with your subconscious mind, encourage fuller dream recall, and allows you to track your dreams. (202)

Dream Re-Entry gives you the ability to go back into a dream through meditation to fix the ending or get clearer insight into what the dream is trying to tell you. (204)

Lucid Dreaming allows you to consciously shift and program your dreams so you can reach better resolutions and gain fuller confidence. (205)

Host a Dream Circle broadens your dream vocabulary by introducing you to other people's dreams. A community experience, dream circles help friendships grow while building emotional and spiritual development. (206)

The Merkabah is a non-physical aspect of your earthly being that balances the masculine and feminine aspects of source and energizes your auric fields. (208)

Astral Travel happens when the soul explores the non-physical aspect of reality, often in the dreamtime. Astral travel is a very freeing experience for many, helping release constricting thought patterns and allowing the mind to bridge space and time. (211)

The Akash is the non-physical blueprint or "control room" for Earth that determines how physical reality comes together. It holds the records of all that will ever be or has been. Visit the Akash to work with past/present/future lives or to work on your own "etheric dashboard" and shift your current reality or enact generational healing through your karmic and genetic bloodline. (219)

Vow Breaking releases unintentional (karmic) and perceived contracts we have made with other people or ourselves which may not be for our highest good (vows of poverty, revenge pacts, etc.) (221)

Fire Ceremony uses the transformative power of fire to release patterns or fears you no longer want to maintain. *Adult supervision required!* (223)

The Temple of Lives is a meditation that allows you to view your other lifetimes (the Akash) so you can release any patterns or negative emotional attachments that no longer serve you. **(mayacointreau.com/transform/lives.mp3)** (225)

TOOLS & USES	Pg.	Energy	Create	Relax	Balance	Intuit	Let Go & Heal
The ABCs	94	✓		✓	✓		
Ahamkara Mudra	9			✓	✓		
Akash	219	✓		✓	✓		✓
Art Booking	148		✓	✓		✓	✓
Astral Travel	211			✓		✓	
Automatic Writing	47		✓			✓	
Bhudi Mudra	9	✓			✓	✓	
Blessing Boxes	74	✓	✓				✓
Body Mapping	134				✓	✓	
Brain Wave Music	15	✓	✓	✓	✓		✓
Breath of Fire	7	✓					
Breath of Moon	7			✓		✓	
Breath of Sun	7	✓	✓				
Bullet Journaling	49		✓	✓	✓		
Chanting	17	✓		✓	✓		✓
Chromotherapy	141	✓		✓	✓		✓
Connect w/ Guides	173			✓		✓	✓
Cord Removal	185	✓					✓
Create A Healing Sanctuary	19		✓	✓			✓
Crystals and Stones	165	✓		✓	✓	✓	✓

TOOLS & USES	Pg.	Energy	Create	Relax	Balance	Intuit	Let Go & Heal
Dream Circles	206			✓		✓	
Dream Journaling	202		✓			✓	✓
Dream Re-Entry	204						✓
Drumming, Rattles and Singing Bowls	96	✓		✓	✓		✓
Earthing	96	✓		✓	✓		
Eating & Sleeping	124	✓		✓	✓		✓
EFT	40			✓			✓
Essential Oils	129	✓		✓	✓		✓
Finger Massage	157			✓	✓		
Fire Ceremony	223	✓	✓				✓
Four-fold Breath	5			✓	✓		✓
Freewriting	44		✓	✓		✓	
Give Yourself a Hug	66			✓			
HA! Airplane	194	✓					
Herbs & Teas	196	✓		✓	✓		✓
Ho'oponopono	69				✓		✓
Hydrochromopathy	143	✓	✓	✓	✓		✓
I AM	79		✓	✓	✓		✓
If It Were Me...	24					✓	✓
Be a Tree	98				✓		✓

TOOLS & USES	Pg.	Energy	Create	Relax	Balance	Intuit	Let Go & Heal
Iris Healing Method™	196	✓					✓
It's All Part of You	37						✓
Kubera Mudra	9		✓		✓		
Kundalini Practice	191	✓					
Light Therapy	140	✓		✓	✓		✓
Loving Kindness	62			✓	✓	✓	✓
Lucid Dreaming	205			✓		✓	
Medicine Wheel	157				✓		
The Merkabah	208	✓			✓		
Mountain Grounding	115			✓	✓		
Mukula Mudra	9				✓		✓
Negative Ions	97	✓		✓			✓
Positive Affirming	65		✓				✓
Positive Boundaries	108			✓	✓		✓
Pyramid Protection	111			✓	✓	✓	
Qigong & Yoga	195	✓		✓	✓		✓
Seat of 4 Elements	159			✓	✓		
Shamanic Journey	182			✓	✓	✓	✓

TOOLS & USES	Pg.	Energy	Create	Relax	Balance	Intuit	Let Go & Heal
Sway Testing	131					✓	✓
Temple of Guidance	178			✓		✓	
Temple of Inspiration	81	✓	✓	✓		✓	
Temple of the Light	187	✓		✓			✓
Temple of Lives	225						✓
Temple of the Open Heart	120			✓			✓
Third Eye Breathing	203			✓		✓	
Tighten Your Silver Cord	106	✓		✓	✓		
Toning & Groaning	17	✓		✓	✓		✓
Trace the Trigger	39						✓
Transfigurational Toning	75	✓	✓		✓		✓
Vision Boards	75	✓	✓				✓
Vow Breaking	221		✓				✓
Woodchopper	194			✓	✓		

A Note to Caregivers & Counselors

The **Teen Transformation Manual** was originally intended as a self-guiding tool for kids and young adults but it has evolved into something much, much more. While many teens find this book helpful to access their spiritual nature and bring their lives into balance, I have been approached by numerous counselors and caregivers about how helpful this manual is as a co-creative tool. Therapists are using the exercises with the kids around them. Parents are meditating and bullet journaling with their children. Relationships are being strengthened and teens are finally feeling heard, cared for, and understood.

Before you do anything with your teen, I suggest reading the introduction and first four chapters and taking some time to let the information digest. If you are a parent or other caregiver, you might enjoy working the book together with your teen after you've read those first few chapters. As a counselor or teacher, the teens under your care will probably benefit most if you read the book all the way through before you begin utilizing the tools here with them. Each chapter builds upon the lessons that come before it, and much of the work within these pages can easily complement other programs.

Don't be discouraged if your teen doesn't seem focused or if they only do pieces of the "work." Teens are hard-wired for multi-tasking and quick analysis, and they often only need a quick glimpse of the truth to internalize it forever. One minute of meditation, ten seconds of serenity – all they need at this point in their lives is some familiarity with the feeling so that they can access it at a later date. Don't push for a full period of chanting, an hour of meditation, or a stringent practice of journaling. There is a lot of information here in this book, knowledge many adults work on accumulating over decades. I've always been a fan of giving people as much information as I can and then allowing them to pick and choose what works for them. While some truths may be universal, knowledge is personal.

At the end of the day, each person's search for fulfilment and peace must be made alone. What works for you may not work for your children. The technique that centers your 10am client may set your 11 o'clock's teeth on edge. Every human, whether teen or adult, is different in both body and spirit. We all have different nervous systems, different genes that determine how we handle disease and stress. The same goes for our emotions and our spirit.

You cannot apply a "one size fits all" solution to the teens in your care and expect it to work for everyone.

The more familiar you are with the theories and exercises in this book, the easier it will be for you to determine which methods will work best in any given situation. Above all, I suggest you try the exercises yourself, because the more centered you are the better you will able to provide your teen with a safe haven. When you are walking the walk, those around you will more easily rise to meet you on your level. Just being in your presence will help your teens find their own equilibrium, and eventually, their own path with a heart.

About the Author

A mother of two, Maya Cointreau is an author and teacher specializing in the holistic health and metaphysical fields. Passionate about all avenues of healing, Maya is particularly interested in the evolving merger of science and spirituality, and its impact upon healthcare and humanity. She has over 20 years of experience in vibrational healing and is an Usui Reiki Master attuned in Karuna Reiki and the Iris Healing Method™, along with having rigorously studied herbalism, flower essences, polarity therapy, naturopathic principles, homeopathy, core shamanism, and aromatherapy.

Her books are published by Earth Lodge®, a company dedicated to producing high quality vibrational healing remedies and publications for body, mind, and spirit. *The Girl Who Could Dance in Outer Space* is used in Houghton Mifflin Harcourt's curriculum in elementary schools worldwide.

When all her other work is put away, Maya runs online short story and poetry competitions with her good friend, Monisha Saldanha Banerjee. Publishing talented authors since 2004, Momaya Press has become a powerful avenue for aspiring writers to connect with real editors and professionals in the industry.

www.ingramcontent.com/pod-product-compliance
Lightning Source LLC
Chambersburg PA
CBHW031949090426
42739CB00006B/123